David Day

My diary of rambles with the 25th Mass. volunteer infantry

18th army corps, and Army of the James

David Day

My diary of rambles with the 25th Mass. volunteer infantry
18th army corps, and Army of the James

ISBN/EAN: 9783337174934

Printed in Europe, USA, Canada, Australia, Japan

Cover: Foto ©ninafisch / pixelio.de

More available books at **www.hansebooks.com**

MY DIARY

OF

RAMBLES WITH THE

25TH MASS. VOLUNTEER INFANTRY,

WITH

BURNSIDE'S COAST DIVISION;

18TH ARMY CORPS,

AND

ARMY OF THE JAMES.

COPYRIGHTED, 1883,

BY D. L. DAY.

KING & BILLINGS, PRINTERS,
GAZETTE OFFICE,
MILFORD, . . MASS.
1884.

INTRODUCTION.

While in the army, I kept a diary of my wanderings, observations and adventures. It was kept in the form of letters sent home, and with notes and memoranda in pocket diaries. It was simply incident and anecdote of what came under my observation, and with what I had to do; and from those letters and memoranda, I have compiled this book.

I had two objects in view in compiling it. The first was, I desired to show to my posterity the heroism, sacrifices, privations and hardships of their illustrious ancestor; to transmit to them a country and a name, and the government of our fathers unimpaired. The other was, that getting a little past the age for labor, and as people have fussy notions in regard to foraging, something had to be done to recruit my commissariat, hence I write a book; and to all the old comrades, and to all purchasers of this book, who thereby help to smooth the cares and wrinkles of my declining years, this little volume is respectfully dedicated

By the Author,

D. L. DAY.

Milford, Mass., February, 1884.

CHAPTER I.

Milford, Mass., Sept. 6, 1861.

THE BEGINNING.

Pursuant to a call from President Lincoln for more troops in suppression of the great rebellion, a regiment is now being recruited in the city of Worcester for that service, and a company is being recruited here for that regiment. Believing that it is too soon to divide the estate, and that too many different administrations running at the same time might run amuck, and believing I should never feel quite satisfied with myself if I do not go, and believing with President Jackson, that the Union must and shall be preserved, I have this day enlisted in the company now being raised here. It would be useless for me to claim that I have enlisted from purely patriotic motives, as no one would believe it; and surely none would believe that I would enlist for the plain thirteen dollars a month. So I may as well call it that I have enlisted partly from a love of adventure; for the other part, people are at liberty to draw their own inferences.

The formation of this company was suggested by Mr. George Draper, a patriotic and public spirited citizen of the town, who has given liberally of his means for its success; his son also enlisting in the company. It has also received the aid and patronage of several other patriotic citizens of the town.

Sept. 24. Captain Clark has received orders to report with his company at Worcester, tomorrow. The thing seems to be becoming a reality.

Sept. 25. Under escort of the Milford Brass Band, we marched through a few of the principal streets to the depot. Here a large concourse of citizens had collected to give us their best wishes, and see us off. We now began to realize some of the discomforts of a soldier's life. There not being passenger cars enough to accommodate us, we were crowded into two box freight cars for South Framingham, where we changed to passenger cars for Worcester. Arriving there, we marched to the city hall, where we took dinner. From there we marched to the agricultural grounds west of the city, where we are to encamp. This camp is named Camp Lincoln, in honor of Ex-Governor Lincoln of Worcester.

Sept. 26. Being the first company on the ground, and not having tents, we bivouacked last night in Agricultural Hall. Sleeping on a hard pine board was new business to most of us, and Morpheus was courted in vain. The boys, however, made a frolic of the night, and more unearthly noises and sounds never greeted my ears. I think the rebels would never need hear the sound of our guns to frighten them, if they could hear sounds like those. Several other companies arrived on the ground this morning, and this afternoon all hands are busy pitching tents.

SEPT. 27. Ten companies are now on the ground. Colonel Upton made us a visit to-day. He is to be our commander. I have known the colonel for several years past at our militia musters. He commanded the old 9th regiment, one which stood second to none in the state. I regard the colonel as a very fine man, and an able military commander. Under his command I have no fears but that our regiment will make a record that not only themselves, but the state will be proud of.

OCT. 7. We were today mustered into the service of the United States, by Captain John M. Goodhue, U. S. A. The company is designated as Company B, and the regiment as the 25th Massachusetts volunteers. I suppose we are now stuck for three years unless sooner shot.

COL. UPTON TAKES COMMAND.

OCT. 8. Col. Upton assumed command of the regiment to-day, and will at once set about perfecting the organization and discipline. The officers are:

FIELD AND STAFF.

Colonel,	Edwin Upton, Fitchburg.
Lieutenant Colonel,	Augustus B. R. Sprague, Worcester.
Major,	Matthew J. Mc Cafferty, Worcester.
Adjutant,	Elijah A. Harkness, Worcester.
Quartermaster,	William O. Brown, Fitchburg.
Surgeon,	J. Marcus Rice, M. D., Worcester.

COMPANY A. Captain, Josiah Picket, Worcester. 1st Lieutenant, Frank E. Goodwin, Worcester. 2d Lieutenant, Merritt B. Bessey, Worcester.

COMPANY B. Captain, Willard Clark, Milford. 1st Lieutenant, William Emery, Milford. 2d Lieutenant, William F. Draper, Milford.

COMPANY C. Captain, Cornelius G. Atwood, Boston. 1st Lieutenant, James Tucker, Boston. 2d Lieutenant, Merrick F. Prouty, Spencer.

COMPANY D. Captain, Albert F. Foster, Worcester. 1st Lieutenant, George S. Campbell, Worcester. 2d Lieutenant, George H. Spaulding, Worcester.

COMPANY E. Captain, Thomas O'Neill, Worcester. 1st Lieutenant, William Daly, Worcester. 2d Lieutenant, Henry McConville, Worcester.

COMPANY F. Captain, Charles H. Foss, Fitchburg. 1st Lieutenant, Levi Lawrence, Fitchburg. 2d Lieutenant, J. Henry Richardson, Fitchburg.

COMPANY G. Captain, Louis Wagely, Worcester. 1st Lieutenant, Henry M. Rickster, Worcester. 2d Lieutenant, Frederic M. Weigand, Worcester.

COMPANY H. Captain, Orson Moulton, Worcester. 1st Lieutenant, David M. Woodward, Worcester. 2d Lieutenant, Nathaniel H. Foster, North Brookfield.

COMPANY I. Captain, Varanus P. Parkhurst, Templeton. 1st Lieutenant, James B. Smith, Royalston. 2d Lieutenant, Amos Buffom, Templeton.

COMPANY K. Captain, J. Waldo Denny, Worcester. 1st Lieutenant, Samuel Harrington, Paxton. 2d Lieutenant, James M. Drennan, Worcester.

Most of these officers and many of the enlisted men have done military duty either in the state militia, or as three-months men around Washington. So we are not an entirely green crowd. The officers are a fine looking body of young men, and I think, with a little flattery and catering to their vanity, we shall get along nicely with them.

OCT. 12. The boys are settling down to the routine of military duty, and getting accustomed to camp life. They take kindly to discipline, and seem anxious to learn the drill.

PRESENTATIONS.

Presentations are the order of the day. The adjutant has had a horse presented him by his firemen friends. A great, stout, clumsy, good-natured horse. I should think he was better adapted for hauling a fire engine than for a parade horse, but perhaps will answer the purpose well enough.

The major's friends have also presented him with a horse. A good kind of horse enough. Nothing very stylish or dashy about him for a war charger, but perhaps he can smell the battle as far as any horse. The major, in a clever little speech, assured his friends that they would never hear of the nag's striking his best gait to the rear. The major being a man of immense rotundity, I imagine that the horse after carrying him a couple of hours, would feel willing to give boot to go into the ranks rather than remain on the staff.

The Worcester ladies, with commendable patriotism, have presented us with a splendid silk banner (the national colors), and have enjoined us to carry it with us in our wanderings, and return it again to them without dishonor. And we have sworn by a thousand stout hearts and bright bayonets, that that banner shall float above the battlements of secession and be again returned to them, crowned with the laurel wreaths of victory. And when amid the flame and thunder of the battle, we look on its bright folds, remembering its fair donors, rush to victory and glory.

SPECULATIONS.

Our time is being occupied with drills and receiving company, with which we are highly favored and are always glad to see. The boys are having leave of absence, and are visiting their homes preparatory for their departure south. Many are the speculations among the boys as to our destination, but no one seems to know anything about it. I tell them I think we shall go to Dixie.

SELECTING A CHAPLAIN.

After hearing several candidates for the office of chaplain, they have finally settled on Rev. Horace James, pastor of the old South church, Worcester. I think they have shown good judgment in selecting a chaplain of the orthodox faith, as no one visiting our camp for an hour could doubt their belief in the existence of the burning lake by the way they consign each other to that locality.

THE LADIES.

The pretty girls, God bless their souls, are always first and foremost in every good work, and they are now in session at Agricultural Hall, busily at work for the soldiers. They are making repairs and alterations in our uniforms, sewing on chevrons and doing whatever small jobs of needlework we may desire. They have also furnished us with needles, thread, wax, buttons, pincushions, pins and other small articles which we may need. For all of which they will please accept the warmest emotions of grateful hearts.

WE LEAVE WORCESTER.

Oct. 31. It seems that at last we have been ordered from these cold, frosty climes, to a warmer and more genial one—the Sunny South. After partaking of a collation furnished by the ladies at the hall, at 3 p. m. we broke camp, and taking all our worldly effects upon our backs, preceded by our band, marched through Highland and Main streets to the common, where we took cars for New York. At the common we were met by a large concourse of citizens, friends and relatives of the regiment, who took us by the hand, giving us words of encouragement and a hearty God bless you.

Here were leave takings that required some nerve to suppress the rising tear. Probably some of us have seen our friends for the last time on earth, and bade them the last good-bye. But we will go forward to duty, trusting in God, and hoping for the best.

WE ARRIVE AT NEW YORK.

Nov. 1. We left Worcester about 5 o'clock last evening. Arriving at Norwich, we went aboard the large and splendid steamer Connecticut, the regiment numbering one thousand and thirty, with all our horses, wagons and camp equipage. The staunch steamer bore us rapidly across the sound, landing us in New York about 9 o'clock this morning.

After disembarking and forming the regiment, we marched amid a perfect storm of applause and the New Yorker's peculiar "hi! hi!" to the City Hall park. A guard was then posted and the regiment dismissed until drum call. A committee of gentlemen waited on the colonel, inviting him, his officers and the band, to a dinner at the Astor House. After they had gone, we fellows, by invitation, marched into the park barracks, to regale ourselves on mutton soup. And in all fairness, I must say that a worse soup or dirtier surroundings never came under my observation. I didn't hanker for any, and beat a hasty retreat. If that soup didn't smell to heaven, it must have attained a high altitude above the city. Fortunate New Yorkers, that dwell in basements. I suppose the evening papers will have it that the 25th Massachusetts regiment dined at the Astor House. So we shall get the name, if we missed the turkey. Feeling inclined to take a stroll and see the sights of the big city (the guards not being very effective), it was an easy matter to break the bounds, and we had things our own way until about 4 o'clock, when the regiment was again formed.

MARCHING DOWN BROADWAY.

With an easy, swinging gait, in column of platoons, we marched down Broadway, looking the very soul of soldiery, and were greeted with a perfect ovation all along the route, until we reached the Jersey City ferry, when we crossed to Jersey City, and took cars for Philadelphia.

A STREAK OF LUCK.

While waiting in the cars at Jersey City, the depot and platforms were crowded with people, all anxious to see and talk with us. Happening to have a seat next to the window, a gentleman engaged me in conversation. He asked all manner of questions about the regiment, and among others, if we were well provided for, meaning, I supposed, with clothing, blankets, rations, etc. I said we seemed to be well provided with everything, except perhaps the sinews of war; in that direction I thought we were rather weak. On hearing that, he drew from the depths of his pantaloons pocket, a couple of half dollars and tendered me, which I accepted with many thanks, and best wishes for his health and happiness. That was true patriotism; good fellow! long may you wave.

BREAKFAST IN PHILADELPHIA.

Nov. 2. Arrived in Philadelphia at 1 a. m.; were met at the depot by a committee of the citizens, and escorted to the old cooper-shop saloon, where we took breakfast. Our reception here was in striking contrast with that in New York, yesterday. Instead of dark, gloomy, dirty barracks, with dirty, insolent attendants, we were taken to a large, clean, well-lighted hall, where we were met by a corps of neat, well-dressed and courteous attendants, both ladies and gentlemen, who seemed to vie with each other in their attentions to our wants. The tables were neatly spread, and contained even more than reasonably hungry men could desire. We had boiled corned beef, tongue, ham, brown and white bread, butter, pies, cake, fruit, tea, coffee, milk, etc. Not satisfied with our eating all we wanted, they emptied our haversacks, and filled them with ham, tongue, bread, cake and apples, remarking at the same time, that soldiers couldn't carry salt mule and hardtack through Philadelphia.

Breakfast over, we then had music by our band, and some short remarks by gentlemen present, after which three cheers were proposed for the Philadelphians, which were given with a will. The regiment now re-formed for a march across the city, to take the cars for Baltimore. As our band struck up the music, waking the echoes of the early morning, the windows on either side flew up, and out peered hundreds of heads, in their scantily arranged toilets, and with wild hurrahs and waving handkerchiefs, cheered us on our way. At 4 a. m., we were aboard the cars and moving towards Baltimore.

I was informed that all troops passing through Philadelphia were received and fed in this same generous manner. It makes no difference when troops arrive, whether day or night, they are ready for them. They seem to find out, either by telegraph or some other way, just when a regiment will arrive. I must needs say that these Philadelphians are a generous, whole souled people. They are worth fighting for, in fact they are the very ace of hearts; may prosperity attend them.

ARRIVAL AT BALTIMORE.

Nov. 3. We reached Havre de Grace about noon. A heavy storm has set in. It is raining hard and the wind blows a gale. We crossed the Susquehanna river at this place, on a big steam ferry boat, and I must confess to some fears, as I looked from the car windows down to the water, a distance of nearly fifty feet, and wondered why we did not capsize. Here I saw a government mule pen. Several acres are enclosed, and I was told that the pen contained about 10,000 mules. A large number of negroes are employed taking care of them. I think this must be a base of supplies. After waiting here an hour or so to make up our train, we again started. An hour's ride brought us to the famous gunpowder bridge, which crosses an arm of Chesapeake bay, not far from Baltimore. This bridge the rebels attempted to burn, and partially succeeded. Many of the charred timbers are still to be seen on the bridge. There we saw the first soldiers on duty, a picket guard being kept here to protect the bridge. We reached Baltimore about 3 p. m., and left the cars in the midst of a drenching rain, and marched about a mile through the rain and wind, to the steamboat landing, the band playing The Campbells Are Coming. No boat being in readiness to take us to Annapolis, Col. Upton told the captains of companies that they must find quarters for their men, and be ready for an early start in the morning. Captain Clark obtained a loft in a grain store for his company, where we passed the night very comfortably.

Nov. 4. Sunday morning in Baltimore, and a stiller or more quiet place I never saw. No sounds are heard, no people or carriages are seen in the street. It looks and seems like a deserted city. We took a hurried glance at a portion of the city, visiting Pratt street, where the assault on the 6th Massachusetts took place. The bullet holes and scars on the walls of the buildings, gave proof that the boys got a good deal interested, while passing through that street.

OFF FOR ANNAPOLIS.

We embarked on the steamer Louisiana, about 9 a. m., for Annapolis. As we steamed past old Fort McHenry, I was reminded of an interesting scrap of history connected with this fort. When the British fleet bombarded this fort during the last war with England, there was aboard one of the ships, an American prisoner, a Mr. Key, I think his name was, who watched with the most intense anxiety, the result of the bombardment, and during its progress, wrote the song that has since become famous as one of our national anthems, The Star Spangled Banner.

"By the cannon's red glare, the bombs bursting in air,
Gave proof through the night, that our flag was still there."

Arrived at Annapolis about noon, and marched up to the Naval academy, where we quartered and took dinner with the 21st Massachusetts, now doing garrison duty at this post.

Religious services this afternoon, by Chaplains Ball of the 21st and James of our own regiment. I cannot say that I was much interested in the meeting, as I was very tired, and preaching about the Pharisees and other antiquated sinners of a thousand years ago, did not seem to apply to my case, or the present time.

CAMP HICKS.

Nov. 5. Went into camp on Taylor's farm, about a mile west of the city, and Col. Upton has christened it Camp Hicks, in honor of Gov. Hicks, the present loyal governor of Maryland. The 51st New York is encamped near by us, and that regiment, with the 21st Massachusetts, were the only troops here before us.

Nov. 11. We are now fairly settled in camp life. Several other regiments from Massachusetts and other states are now with us, and drills, inspections and reviews are the order of the day. One can scarcely get time to wash his face, and take, as Gen. Scott said, a hasty plate of soup, before the drum calls to some kind of duty.

Nov. 16. Here it is the middle of November, and the weather is most delightful. No frosts, but a warm, mellow atmosphere like our Indian summer in October. It is beautiful, indeed; I am charmed with it. While our farmers in New England are putting up and feeding their cattle in barns, the cattle here are luxuriating in white clover, young, sweet and tender enough to suit the most fastidious taste of any of the cattle on a thousand hills. The farmers about here are harvesting their crops of corn and sweet potatoes, some of which are very fine. Some of the boys brought in some egg plants which grow about here. I never saw any before, but am told they are very good, when properly cooked. I am not disposed to doubt it, never having eaten any of them, but I cannot believe they would make good egg nog.

We begin to see a little something of the peculiar institution, —slavery. There are a great many negroes strolling around the camps, most of them runaways, and as Maryland is supposed to be a loyal state, we have no right to take sides and afford them protection. But we have adopted a kind of English neutrality, although not giving them much protection, we give them whatever information they desire. The masters and hunters are frequently here, looking up their boys, as they call them, and we generally manage to put them on the wrong track and then run the boys into other camps, and they run them into the woods.

Our regiment was yesterday inspected and reviewed by Brig. Gen. John G. Foster. We put in our best work, and tried to make the best appearance we could. The general seems to be a man who understands his business. At a single glance he takes a man and his equipments all in; looks at his rifle, passes it back and goes for the next one. He complimented Col. Upton on the good drill and appearance of his regiment, and flattered his vanity a little by telling him that with a little more practice his regiment would be as near regulars as it would be possible to bring a volunteer regiment.

Nov. 20. Yesterday, having a day to myself, I visited Annapolis. I was greatly interested in visiting the old State House on account of the historic memories that cluster around it. I was shown up in the hall where Washington, in December, 1783, resigned his commission in the army to the Continental congress, then in session at this place. His resignation was a very solemn and formal affair, and as I stood in this venerable hall, my thoughts went back to those grand old days when our fathers struggled for independence. At the close of the revolution, Maryland offered to cede Annapolis as the Federal capital, but it was thought best to select a site on the Potomac river. Annapolis was originally designed as a great place, being the capital of the state, and possessing a fine harbor with a great depth of water, and long before Baltimore was at all noted, was the seat of wealth, refinement and extensive trade; but it is now chiefly distinguished as the seat of the United States Naval academy. The state house and Episcopal church are located in the centre of the city, and from these radiate all the streets.

To the eye of the stranger, the antique, moss-covered and vine-clad houses, with their deep embrasured windows and peculiar architecture, present a singular appearance. The Naval academy and Episcopal college present a striking contrast to the rest of the town. The buildings are large and of modern style, the grounds around them spacious and tastefully laid-out. The Naval academy, located on the west side of the town, comprises an area of several acres, enclosed by a high brick wall. The buildings, of which there are several, are located partly on the water side, the balance on the east side next to the wall. The wharfage and boat houses are extensive and commodious. On the north side, and commanding the harbor, is an old brick building with a few port holes, and mounting a few old iron guns. This they call the fort, and I should suppose a few shots from one of our gunboats would level it to the ground. The park is beautifully laid out with drives and walks, and adorned with a great variety of forest and ornamental trees. The grounds and trees, however, are being sadly damaged by the soldiers and by driving army wagons across.

Here are also several handsome monuments erected in memory of departed naval heroes, among which I may mention one erected in honor of the gallant Capt. Herndon. It is a plain granite shaft, about twenty feet high, and on each of the four sides is engraved simply the name, Herndon. I noticed this more particularly, as I remembered the circumstances of his death. He ranked as lieutenant in the navy, but at the time of his death, in September, 1857, was in command of the steamer Central America, of the New York and California line. The Central America was on her passage from Aspinwall for New York, when she foundered during a terrible storm off Cape Hatteras, and out of 600 persons on board, only 200 were saved. Capt. Herndon superintended the getting off of as many of his passengers as he could, and the last words he was heard to utter were, "I will never leave the ship until my passengers are all off," and standing on the wheel house, went down with his vessel. Brave, gallant Herndon!

Nov. 22. The first death in our regiment occurred this morning. John Shepard of Company B died of typhoid fever. His remains will be sent to his home in Milford for burial.

THANKSGIVING.

Nov. 30. According to the customs of our Puritan Fathers, last Thursday was observed in Massachusetts and other states as a day of thanksgiving to God, for his manifold mercies and bounties to the erring children of men. The day was observed here throughout all the camps as a holiday. All drills were suspended, and in our camp religious services were held, after which the boys engaged in ball playing and other amusements to which their inclinations might lead. Although deprived of joining our friends at home in their festivities and meeting them around the dear old board, it seems we were not forgotten. Our thanksgiving dinners are just beginning to arrive, and our camp is literally piled up with boxes and bales containing good things from the dear ones at home.

THE TROOPS BRIGADED.

Dec. 2. The troops encamped around here have been formed into three brigades, and will be commanded by Brigadier Generals Foster, Reno and Parke; the whole to be under command of Gen. A. E. Burnside and known as Burnside's coast division. Our regiment has been assigned the right of the first brigade, comprising the 25th, 23d, 24th and 27th Massachusetts and 10th Connecticut regiments, under command of Brig. Gen. John G. Foster, U. S. A. I think we are fortunate in our commander, as he appears to me like a man who understands his business. Gen.

Foster is a regular army officer, ranking as captain of engineers. He served in the Mexican war, and was with Major Anderson at the storming and surrender of Fort Sumpter. He has recently been commissioned brigadier general of volunteers. Judging from appearances, I have great faith in him as an able commander.

COURTS MARTIAL.

DEC. 5. Courts martial seems to be a prominent feature in camp affairs just at present, and almost every night at dress parade the charges and specifications are read against some unlucky wight. The burden of the song seems to be too drunk to perform the duties of a soldier; but as this is a camp of instruction, I presume these courts are really more for practice than anything else.

A WALK INTO THE COUNTRY.

DEC. 10. The weather holds warm and springlike. We have no need of overcoats, unless doing guard duty nights. The people here tell us it is an unusually mild fall, but that we shall get right smart lots of cold and snow before many days. I took a walk of a few miles into the country yesterday, on a tour of observation. I noticed what appeared to me a great extent of good land, but very badly improved. Occasionally I saw a farm where things seemed to be kept up snug and showed some evidences of thrift, but more of them looked as though the owners studied to see how shiftless they could be and still manage to live. Buildings and fences are going to decay; fields of corn are yet unharvested, the cattle and hogs running through and destroying them. I asked one man why he didn't harvest his corn. "Oh," he said, "there is no hurry about that, I have got all winter to do it in, and the corn is just as well off in the field as anywhere." I came to the conclusion that his plan of harvesting was about as fast as he wanted it to eat. I said to another man I met, "You have good land about here, sir; easy of cultivation and close to a market. I suppose you make a pile of money?" "Oh, no," he said, "you are mistaken; right poor land about yere, one can hardly make a living on it, but you go over yere a few miles to some creek [the name of which I have forgotten], and you will find right good land; make as much again corn on it as you can on this." I asked, "What do you value this land at?" "Well," he replied, "we reckon the land around yere worth about $10 an acre; reckon some of it mought be bought for a little less, but the land around Annapolis is worth from $25 to $50 an acre." I made up my mind that a man with an ordinary degree of enterprise, with our improved implements for farming and with hired labor, might take this land and make money on it. I am unable to see any profits from slave labor in Maryland; it is poor help at the best; besides they have to be clothed and fed several months in a year during which time they are not earning much, and there is always on a farm employing a dozen or more field hands, a lot of old men and women and small children who are no earning anything, but still have to be supported.

A LOOK THROUGH THE CAMPS.

Dec. 18. I have been looking through the camps around here and am astonished at the amount of offal and swill that is buried up and lost instead of being turned to a valuable account. An enterprising farmer could collect from these camps, manure and swill to the value of $100 a day, costing nothing but simply carting it off, thus enriching his land and fattening hundreds of hogs and cattle; but this lack of energy and enterprise prevents these people from turning anything to account. They content themselves with sitting down and finding fault with the government and their more enterprising and energetic neighbors of the north.

A DEPOT OF SUPPLIES.

Dec. 20. We are having cold weather; freezing quite hard at night, and making our lodgings in these little rag houses anything but comfortable. I have been with a detail of men down to the wharf unloading and storing army supplies. Annapolis is a depot of supplies, and immense quantities are landed here and sent by rail to Washington. A person never having given the subject of army preparation and supplies much thought, would be astonished at the immense quantities he would see here, and would begin to calculate how long it would be before Uncle Sam would be bankrupt. Large warehouses are filled and breaking down under the weight of flour, beef, pork, bread, sugar, coffee, clothing, ammunition, etc., while the wharves and adjacent grounds are filled with hay, oats, lumber, coal, guns, mortars, gun-carriages, pontoons and other appendages of an army. I presume the cost of feeding and clothing an army of half a million of men is not really so much as the same number of men would cost at home, but the army being consumers, instead of producers, the balance will eventually be found on the debit page of the ledger.

CHRISTMAS.

Dec. 24. To morrow will be Christmas, and the boys in all the camps are making great preparations for the coming event. The camps are being put in order and decorated with evergreens. Some of them are trimmed in good taste and look very neat and pretty. The boys are all looking forward to a good time; I hope they will not be disappointed. Santa Claus is expected here tonight with our Christmas dinners, but he may be delayed and not get here for a week to come.

Dec. 26. Christmas went off very pleasantly and apparently to the satisfaction of all. Drills were suspended and all went in for a good time. The Irishmen had their Christmas box, the Germans their song and lager, while ball playing and other athletic sports used up the day, and music and dancing were the order of the evening. Santa Claus came with a Christmas dinner for a few, but more of us he passed by; however, I think the old gentleman has got a store for us somewhere on the way.

Our camp was visited by a number of ladies and gentlemen from the city, who were guests at headquarters, Chaplain James doing the polite, and entertaining them as best he could. No farther south than this, I was surprised to hear the chaplain tell of the ignorance of these people in regard to northern people and their institutions. One lady, noticing a box of letters in the chaplain's tent, said she thought he must have a very large correspondence to have so many letters. He told her those were soldiers' letters going home to their friends. "Why," she asked, "are there many of your soldiers who can write?" He informed her that there were not a half dozen men in the regiment but could read and write. He told her that free schools were an institution at the north. No man was so poor but he could educate his children, and the man who neglected their education was regarded as little better than the brutes. The lady appeared quite astonished and said she thought our free schools were only for the rich.

RUMORS.

DEC. 28. The camp is full of rumors about our leaving, but I hardly think any one knows much about it as yet, although it is quite probable we shall leave before long. The expedition is all here and has been perfected in drill. Nothing that I can see prevents us from leaving at any time. When we break this camp we can count our happy time over, that we have seen our best days of soldiering. Campaign life in the field, as I understand it, is at the best a life of hardship, privation and danger, and the man who expects much else, will be grievously disappointed.

A DULL DAY.

JAN. 1, 1862. The new year is ushered in with a light fall of snow and very cold weather. There is just snow enough to prevent drills or any sports the boys may have been anticipating. Altogether the day will be a dull one. The sutler, anticipating our removal, has not much to sell or steal. The sutler is regarded as the common enemy of the soldier, and when forced contributions are levied on him it is considered entirely legitimate and rather a good joke. The boys will have to content themselves with card playing and writing letters home. We have just got a new stove running in my tent, and Long Tom is detailed today to supply it with wood. I think we shall make a comfortable day of it, if Tom does his duty. Things certainly begin to look like leaving; the harbor is full of vessels, transports, gunboats and supply ships. Appearances indicate that somebody will hear it thunder somewhere along the southern coast before very long.

ORDERS TO LEAVE.

JAN. 5. Orders have been issued to break camp and go aboard the transports tomorrow morning. The boys are now breaking the frozen ground around the tent pins, packing their knapsacks and getting ready for a start. We have been here so long it seems almost like leaving home to break up and go out on untried scenes.

CHAPTER II.

JAN. 6. Reveille beat at 6 o'clock this morning, and all hands turned out in the midst of a driving snow storm, elated at the prospect of getting away. I cannot say I was very exuberant in spirit as there was work in it and things began to look like a reality. An hour or so sufficed to pick up our traps and load our camp equipage on the wagons, drink a cup of hot coffee and declare ourselves ready to march. The companies were formed in their company streets, the rolls called, and we marched out on the parade ground and formed the regimental line. Col. Upton said he should like to fire a few rounds as a parting salute to old Camp Hicks, and gave the order to load. The firing over, there came the order, "By companies right wheel! forward march!" and we turned our backs on our old home. Passing the camp of the 27th Massachusetts, we halted, and, wheeling into line, honored them with a salute of a few rounds, which was responded to with hearty cheers. We then marched to the Naval academy, where seven companies, with the field and staff, their horses, band and all the camp equipage, went aboard the steamer New York. Two companies, D and H, went aboard the gunboat Zouave, and company I aboard the schooner Skirmisher. All aboard, the New York steamed out into the harbor a short distance and anchored till further orders.

AN INCIDENT.

A little incident here occurred showing the good nature of Col. Upton. While waiting for the baggage to be got aboard, a small party of us thought we would go up to the academy grounds, and see the 4th Rhode Island boys who had just arrived. We had not been there fifteen minutes before we saw the boat leaving the wharf, and the way we put for it was a caution to travelers a little too late for the cars. We reached the wharf all out of breath, and the first man we saw was Col. Upton. He appeared a little cross at first, and then putting on one of his good-natured looks, asked us where we had been. We replied we had been up to see the Rhode Island boys. "Well," he said, "yonder goes the boat, what are you going to do?" Some one suggested that under the circumstances we had better stand by the colonel and take our chances. "Ah!" he replied, "I will soon have you fellows where I shall know where to find you." He then procured a boat and crew, told us to get aboard and put for the steamer. As we pushed away from the wharf, we left the colonel standing there, looking as good natured and happy as though it was Sunday afternoon and he had just heard a good sermon.

ABOARD THE NEW YORK.

Jan. 7. Here we are, packed like sardines in a box; three companies of us, K, C and B, in the after cabin. The officers and band occupy the saloon and state rooms on the upper deck, the other companies fill the cabin on the forward deck, the ladies' saloon and gangway amidships. The horses are forward, and the baggage is piled up forward and on the guards. Altogether, we are settled in here pretty thick, but by keeping ourselves in good humor and by a little forbearance and accommodation, one to the other, we shall manage to get along and live together in peace, like Barnum's happy family. This boat is a large, first-class steamer, built in the strongest manner and designed for a sea-going boat. She is commanded by Capt. Clark; the first mate is a Mr. Mulligan. Both have the appearance of gentlemen. The troops are embarking as rapidly as possible, and in a day or two more the expedition will be ready to sail.

Jan. 9. As bright and lovely a morning as ever dawned on Chesapeake bay. The expedition sails today. The harbor is full of life, tugboats are running in all directions, vessels are getting themselves in their order in line, the anchors are all up and waiting the signal gun to start.

10 a. m. The signal gun announces that all is ready for the departure of the expedition. Slowly the flag-boat, containing Gen. Burnside and staff, moves off, followed by other boats as fast as they get ready to sail. Nothing particular occurred during the day's sail. The bay is wide and we were so far from either shore that we could distinguish nothing of interest. We passed the mouth of the Potomac river a little before sunset, and shortly after dropped anchor for the night.

Jan. 10. A thick, heavy fog envelopes the bay this morning, so thick we cannot see half the boat's length. In a little while the fog began to settle, and it looked curious to see the topmasts of the boats and schooners above the fog as they passed us, their hulls being hidden entirely from view.

9 a. m. Weighed anchor and proceeded on our journey. Our boat being first after the flag-boat, we soon passed the boats that ran by us in the fog.

ARRIVAL AT FORTRESS MONROE.

A little before noon we sighted Fortress Monroe, and as we passed the Minnesota and other men-of-war lying in the roads, the sailors sprang into the rigging and cheered lustily, to which the boys responded heartily from the boats, the bands playing as each boat passed.

At 12 m., our boat dropped anchor between the rip raps and the fort. Every available place on the boat for sight seeing was quickly taken, the boys eagerly looking at things the like of which they never saw before, and many of them probably never supposed existed.

Here it appears is the rendezvous of the expedition; gunboats, tugboats and supply vessels in great numbers are lying here to join us. If one-half the armada lying here accompany us, we may naturally conclude there is heavy work to be done somewhere, or else we are taking force enough to break down all opposition and make an easy job of it.

JAN. 11. As I look out on the Old Dominion, the Mother of presidents, statesmen and heroes, my mind is filled with historical reminiscences of its past greatness and glory. Alas! that Virginia, a state that bore such a proud record in the history of our country, a state that has done so much and sacrificed so much to gain our independence and establish our government, should now be sunk in the mire and slough of rebellion.

There is no appearance of leaving here today; many of the officers are going ashore to look around, and the boys are amusing themselves as best they can. Many and various are the speculations and conjectures as to our destination. Some think we are to make an attack on Yorktown, others that Norfolk is the point of attack. Some prophesy that we shall go up the James river, others that we are going far down the coast. I have not bothered myself much about it, but conclude we shall fetch up somewhere. As one looks on "old glory" proudly waving over the frowning battlements of Fortress Monroe and the rip raps, he would naturally conclude that this part of Virginia had not passed the ordinance of secession. Fortress Monroe is built of granite and earthworks, and is calculated, I believe, to mount some 400 or 500 guns. It is the largest and strongest fort on the coast and the only complete work in this country; hence it is called a fortress. The rip raps is an unfinished work, built on an artificial island, and situated about a mile east of Fortress Monroe. When completed, it will be a powerful work, and all vessels going to Norfolk or up the James river will have to pass between the two forts.

Looking west we can see the ruins of Hampton, burned last fall by order of Gen. Magruder. Speaking of Magruder reminds me of an anecdote I have somewhere read of him. While serving in Mexico, he ranked as captain of infantry in the regular army. While there he was in the habit of spreeing it pretty hard, and early one morning, after he had been out on a pretty rough time, his regiment received orders to march. By some strange oversight, the captain failed to replenish his canteen, and in a little while he began to experience an intolerable thirst. In this dilemma he called on one of his privates, whom he supposed might have something, and asked him what he had in his canteen. He was told that it contained a certain kind of Mexican liquor, of which the captain was very fond. After taking a pretty good bumper, he said, "Private Jones, you will hereafter rank as corporal, and be obeyed and respected as such." After a while, his thirst again coming on, he goes and calls for some more of the liquor. This time he about found the bottom of the canteen, and thanking the corporal for his politeness, said to him, "Corporal Jones, you will hereafter rank as sergeant, and be obeyed and respected as such." And, as the story went, if the canteen had held out a while longer, private Jones might have ranked as brigadier general.

THE EXPEDITION SAILS.

JAN. 12. The big expedition, with colors flying and bands playing, sailed this afternoon, heading seaward. No one on board will know our destination until we round Cape Henry, when the seals are to be broken. A little before night we passed Cape Henry and headed south. We are now fairly at sea; the wind is blowing hard and the schooners are going past us as though we were anchored. Night has settled down on us and darkness covers the face of the deep. There is nothing more to be seen, we are now the creatures of chance, with the chances against us, and we must learn to adapt ourselves to the circumstances by which we are surrounded. Acting on this philosophy, we will lie down on our hard bunks and listen to the splashing of the water against the sides of our boat.

AT ANCHOR.

JAN. 13. Going on deck this morning, I found we were riding at anchor in sight of Hatteras light. Not knowing the meaning of this, I inquired of Mr. Mulligan if people went out to sea and anchored nights? He laughed and said the shoals and the lights being down along shore made navigation in these waters rather dangerous, and they thought they had better anchor. I went forward to take in the situation. The wind was blowing fresh from the southeast, with heavy swells running. As they weighed anchor, the boat rose and fell with the swells. I rather enjoyed this and thought it very nice. After a few moments I began to experience a peculiar sensation around the waistbands, and it occurred to me that I had better go and lie down. After a half hour I was all right again, and went on deck. Mr. Mulligan said, "We are going to have a great storm and Hatteras is a bad place to be caught in a storm." But by way of encouragement he tells us we are safer with him aboard the New York than we should be at home in bed.

THE STORM AT HATTERAS INLET.

At 1 p. m., we dropped anchor in front of the battery at Hatteras inlet, in the midst of a terrific southeast storm. Our fleet comprising nearly 100 sail are making the inlet as fast as possible; but it is feared that some of them will not be able to get in and will either be lost or have to put back. This is indeed the grandest, wildest scene I ever beheld! As far as the eye can reach, the water is rolling, foaming and dashing over the shoals, throwing its white spray far into the air, as though the sea and sky met. This is no time for man to war against man. The forces of Heaven are loose and in all their fury, the wind howls, the sea rages, the eternal is here in all his majesty. As one looks out on the grand yet terrible scene, he can but exclaim, "Great and marvelous are thy works, Lord, God Almighty!"

A WRECK.

A large steamer, attempting to run in this afternoon, run on the shoals and will probably prove a wreck. As she came in sight and attempted the passage of the inlet, we watched her with breathless anxiety, until she seemed to have passed her greatest danger and all were hopefully looking for her safe arrival, when suddenly she struck the shoal and turned broadside toward us, the sea breaking over her. A shudder ran through the crowd and disappointment was on every countenance. Tugs were immediately dispatched to her assistance, but returned unable to render her any. Capt. Clark thinks if she does not break up during the night, and the wind lulls, that perhaps in the morning she can be got off, or at least those on board of her can. It is not known whether she contains troops or stores. If she should go to pieces during the night, God help those on board of her, as there is no one here that can.

Jan. 14. This morning presents a scene of terror and wildest grandeur. The wrecked steamer has not broken up, but has settled down in the sand, the sea breaking over her, and her rigging is full of men. Boats that have been sent to her assistance are returning, having been unable to render any. We learn from the returning boats that she is the City of New York, loaded with stores. Another tug, with Gen. Burnside and a crew of picked men, has just gone to their assistance, and it is hoped will be able to take them off. The general is not one to see his men perish, and make no effort to rescue them. I reckon our friends at home, when they hear of the loss of this boat, will confound it with our own, and will experience the greatest anxiety until they get our letters, or get righted through the papers. The tug returned this afternoon, bringing off the officers and crew of the wrecked steamer, who report that she is breaking up, and will soon go to pieces.

AT THE MERCY OF THE WIND AND WAVES.

The wind is still blowing a gale. Many of our boats and vessels which have arrived are parting their cables and dragging their anchors, are being driven ashore, or sinking or fouling with each other. The saloon and upper works of our boat are stove in from gunboats and schooners fouling with us. One of our anchor cables has parted, and the engine is slowly working, helping the other one. Many of our vessels are still outside, and fears are entertained that some of them will be lost.

Capt. Clark says no boat can get in here today without the most skilful pilot, and then at great risk of being lost. The gunboat Zouave, with companies D and H of our regiment aboard, is in a sinking condition. Tugs are alongside of her, and the boys are scratching for their lives to get aboard of them. This is the kind of soldiering that makes the boys think of home and of their mothers. I cannot help laughing just a little when a boat or schooner fouls with us, and the timbers and planks begin to crack, to see the boys come out of their bunks, their eyes sticking out of their heads, and rush up stairs to see what the matter is. Well, it is not strange that these young boys should feel a little nervous, as it takes a man of pretty strong nerve to keep his fears down. We are here and have got to make the best of it. If we are to be lost, all our fears will avail us nothing; we must take things coolly, trusting in Providence, Mr. Mulligan and the good old steamer for safety.

JAN. 15. Rough weather still continues, and we are out of rations, subsisting entirely on hardtack and a short ration of that. Unless it calms down so a tug can get alongside, we shall be entirely out in a day or two more. Three more boats dragged their anchors and went ashore this morning, and other boats, with their flags union down, are calling for help. In fact, things are beginning to look gloomy, but amidst all the trouble and discouragements. Gen. Burnside is everywhere to be seen, flying about among the boats and vessels, encouraging his men and looking as cheerful as though everything was going to suit him. Today a rebel boat came down the sound to take a look at us. One of our boats went out to meet her, but the rebel, not caring for an interview, hauled off. The colonel, surgeon and one other man of the 9th New Jersey regiment were drowned today, by the upsetting of a small boat they were in. And so we go, trouble and dangers by sea, and I suppose there will be more by land, if we ever get there.

MORE BOATS ASHORE AND SINKING.

JAN. 16. Three more boats ashore and leaking, one of them is the U. S. mail-boat Suwanee, from Fortress Monroe for Hilton Head. She ran in here this morning to leave mails and dispatches for this fleet, intending to sail this afternoon, but owing to the high winds and heavy sea, she parted her cable and drifted on an anchor fluke, breaking a hole in her bottom and sunk. She lies on the sand, with her deck about four feet out of water. It is said she can be pumped out and raised when it calms, of which time, however, there seems to be a very dim prospect. We have just heard from the old steamer Pocahontas. She went ashore below Hatteras light. She had our team horses aboard, and nearly all of them were lost. The men who were aboard of her got ashore and are now coming down the island. The schooner on which thesignal corps were aboard has not been seen or heard from and there is much anxiety for her safety. We have kept alive on hardtack thus far, but on account of the storm no tug has been able to get alongside with rations, and we going it with half a ration of hardtack and coffee once a day. Five cents apiece are freely offered for hardtack, with no takers.

THE STORM OVER.

JAN. 17. The great storm has at last subsided and the sun once more shines out. All the hands are out playing, everything is putting on a more cheerful appearance, and we can now look around and see the result of the storm. Boats and vessels are ashore all around us, in a partially wrecked or damaged condition. The upper works of our boat are little better than a wreck, from the bowsprits of schooners and catheads of other craft that have fouled with us. Our accommodations are rather limited as is also the fare, but by practicing forbearance and great good nature, the harmony is as perfect as could be expected. A tug is alongside with rations, so at last the long fast is broken. I think the boys will not be over nice about their dinners when they get them. I have sometimes thought I could relish a dinner from that soup I saw at the park barracks. Our dinner today was served about 2 p. m.; bill of fare, pea soup and coffee. I have always persuaded myself that I didn't like pea soup and wouldn't eat it, but today I changed my mind and thought I never ate anything that tasted quite so good as pea soup. I voted it a great luxury.

HATTERAS ISLAND AND INLET.

JAN. 19. Witnessing boat collisions and wrecks is getting old, and the boys are amusing themselves by writing letters, making up their diaries, playing cards, reading old magazines and newspapers which they have read half a dozen times before; and some of them are actually reading their Bibles. Of all the lonely, God-forsaken looking places I ever saw this Hatteras island takes the premium. It is simply a sand-bar rising a little above the water, and the shoals extend nearly 100 miles out to sea. The water is never still and fair weather is never known; storms and sea gulls are the only productions. Sometimes there is a break in the clouds, when the sun can get a shine through for a few moments, but this very rarely happens. The island extends from Cape Henry, Virginia, to Cape Lookout, North Carolina, with occasional holes washed through it, which are called inlets. It is from one-half to two miles wide, and the only things which make any attempt to grow, are a few shrub pines and fishermen. I don't think there is a bird or any kind of animal, unless it is a dog, on the island, not even a grasshopper, as one would have to prospect the whole island to find a blade of grass, and in the event of his finding one would sing himself to death. The inlet is very narrow, not over half a mile in width, and the channel is still narrower, consequently it makes an indifferent harbor. Still it is better than none, or as the sailors say, any port in a storm. But as bad as it looks and bad as it is, it is, after all, a very important point, perhaps as important in a military point of view as any on the coast. It is the key or gate-way to nearly all of eastern North Carolina, and places us directly in the rear of Norfolk, Va. This island is not without its history, if we may believe all the fearful and marvelous stories that have been written of it, of its being the habitation of wreckers and buccaneers in ye good old colony times.

THEATRICALS.

The boys are up to all sorts of inventions to kill time. In the amusement line the officers have started an exhibition or theatre up in the saloon. It is a clever device to break the dull monotony; to cheer up the loneliness and homesickness which seem to prevail. The exercises consist of recitations, dialogues, singing and music, and make a very good evening's entertainment. A limited number from each company are nightly admitted, and I can see no reason why it will not prove a success, as there seems to be no lack of talent, music or patronage. For a comic performance, one should be down in the after-cabin of an evening, especially about the time the officer of the day, who is a lieutenant, comes around to silence the noise and order the lights out. This after-cabin is a sort of independent community, having its own by-laws, and throwing off pretty much all restraint and doing about as it pleases. The officer of the day is pretty sure to keep out of the cabin during the day, but comes to the head of the stairs in the evening, and gives his orders. Very little attention will be given them, until finally he will venture down stairs, when he will be greeted by an hundred voices with, "Officer of the day! turn out the guard!" And a hundred more will respond, "Never mind the guard!" and this will be kept up until they finally drive him out. Sometimes, after the officer of the day has failed to restore order, the colonel will come to the stairs and say, "Boys, it is getting late; time to be quiet." That is the highest known authority, and order will come out of confusion immediately. Without any disparagement to the lieutenants, the boys have a great respect for Col. Upton; he has only to speak and his wishes are cheerfully and instantly complied with.

A QUIET DAY.

Jan. 21. The weather still continues in an unsettled state. Although not so rough as it was, it is still too rough to attempt to do much. All the vessels of our fleet are now here, except those that were lost and the schooner with the signal corps.

MY DIARY.

Nothing has been heard from her, and we are beginning to think that she too may be lost. Albert Tucker of company B died this morning, and his body was taken ashore and buried on the beach this afternoon. It is a sad sight to see men die and be buried here on this low, lonely sand-bar.

> He lies on the beach, the cold waters beside,
> And lonely and sad was the death that he died.
> No mother mourns o'er him, no fond fair one weeps
> Where far from the land of his fathers he sleeps.
> But the mad swelling waves and the wild birds career
> O'er the wet sandy grave of the young volunteer.

HUNTING A CHANNEL.

JAN. 22. The light-draught boats are engaged in finding and making a channel across the bar, or swash as it is called, of sufficient depth of water to enable the large steamers to cross into the sound. One great trouble about that is if they find one today it will all be filled up tomorrow. We shall have to wait till calmer weather before we can cross.

RATIONS.

A schooner came alongside today and left us rations of steamed pork, hardtack and condensed sea water. This was a very timely arrival as we have been very short of water for two or three days and pretty much everything else. Rattlesnake pork will taste pretty good again after a few days' fast. Condensed sea water is rather a disagreeable beverage, but still is a little ahead of no water at all. I think, however, it might be made palatable by adding about nine parts whiskey to one of water. This water and pork is all manufactured here on the spot. They have a sort of rendering establishment where they make it, but I cannot believe that the pork would take a premium in any fair in the country unless it was for meanness.

A RIPPLE OF EXCITEMENT.

Another rebel steamer came down the sound to-day to take a look at us and see how we are getting along. One of our boats gave chase and I reckon got a shot at her, as we heard reports of artillery. Those fellows are just smart enough to keep out of our way, I hope they will always be so, I have no great desire to shoot the cusses, but still if they get in my way, and I think they ought to be shot, I suppose I shall do it.

The theatre up in the saloon is a great success. They have just got out a new play, a kind of burlesque, entitled the Rasper Brothers, and large posters are sent over the boat announcing the unprecedented success of the Rasper Brothers; playing nightly to crowded houses and hundreds turned away; none should fail of witnessing this highly moral drama.

OLD DAN.

Old Dan is having a terrible fit of the blues. He cannot understand why we were sent to this God-forsaken place. I tell him that God has not forsaken it but has sent us here to save it; and Dan, with a big oath, swore that it was not worth saving. I said to him: "You are seeing it at its worst. This is a famous watering-place; a great summer resort." He thinks it might do first-rate for a *watering* place; but cannot conceive of anyone who would want to resort here. He thinks the greatest mistake he has made in this whole business was in not running away as I advised him to, while at Annapolis.

ANOTHER STORM.

Jan. 23. Another great storm. The wind is blowing a gale and the sea is dashing, foaming and threatening everything with destruction. The camps on shore are flooded, the soldiers driven into the fort or up the island; more vessels ashore and the fleet going to the devil. A great many of the men are beginning to despond, and in fact the success of the expedition begins to look gloomy enough. Nothing but hardship and disaster has attended us since we left Fortress Monroe, and God only knows when it will end. Almost any other man but Gen. Burnside would be ready to give it up as a failure; but he is everywhere to be seen, looking cheerful and confident, and encouraging his men. He is a man of indomitable energy, perseverance and courage. He knows no such word as fail, and is bound to overcome all obstacles and dangers.

If the general, by the blessing of God, gets the expedition out of this scrape, and is successful where he strikes, it will give him great prestige, and he will be thought competent for any command. Our engine is slowly working, helping the anchor cable, and Mr. Mulligan says if the other boats will stick to their mudhooks and keep clear of us we shall ride it out all safe. I really hope they will for I am tired of these cathead drills. I have always had rather of a desire for a sea voyage, but I am willing to confess that that wish is fully gratified. This being "rocked in the cradle of the deep" sounds all very pretty in song and romance, but the romance is played out with me, and I think the person who wrote the song,

"A Life on the Ocean Wave."

must have been a proper subject for a lunatic asylum.

Jan. 24. The storm has subsided somewhat, but is still rough enough for all practical purposes. Mr. Mulligan says fair weather *has been known here*, and taking that as a precedent, we may naturally conclude it perhaps *may* be again. This is certainly the longest storm I ever remember of, and never read of but one that exceeded it. That was the one Old Noah got caught out in, but he had the advantage of us, as his was the only craft afloat, and had plenty of sea room; besides his style of navigation was ahead of ours, as he let her drift around where she pleased and trusted to luck for a landing. That kind of navigation might have answered for those times, but would never do for Hatteras.

And now another trouble has happened, the theatre has collapsed, and I am at a loss to understand the reason for it. It certainly could not have been from any lack of talent, music or patronage. It seemed to be perfect in all its appointments, and I can account for its sudden closing in no other way than that there must have been some little indiscretion on the part of the management; but perhaps Rasper Brothers may have had something to do about it. I am sorry it has closed, as I could spend an evening up there very pleasantly. But in the loss of the theatre we must console ourselves with the thought that the drama has always had its difficulties.

THE STORM OVER.

JAN. 25. The storm is at last over, for to-day at least. It has cleared off warm and pleasant, and is the first bright day since we came here. Business is brisk to-day; all is bustle and hurry. There is quite a change of scene, the boats' decks are covered with soldiers, shouting and cheering each other; the bands are all out playing, and altogether it is quite a contrast to the miserable life we have been living. Our attention is taken up watching the operations going on in the harbor, among the shipping. Steamers are being towed across the swash into the sound, and steamers and tugs are at work straining every nerve to pull off the boats that are ashore. It makes fun for the boys watching them pull. Five or six steamers and tugs are at work trying to pull off the Eastern Queen, on which are the 4th Rhode Island boys, and when they all pull together it seems as though they would pull her in two. Sometimes she seems to start a little, and then stick again; the boats will give a steady pull for an hour before she will start again. Occasionally a big cable will break, and it is fun to watch the agility of the boys, dodging the recoil of the cable ends.

The big steamer Northerner attempted to cross the sound at flood tide this morning, and stuck in the middle. She carries the 21st Massachusetts, and I think they will have to be taken off before she can get across. A number of boats and tugs are at work, trying to pull her across. If the Northerner sticks, going across at high water, how we are to cross is a problem yet to be solved, as the New York draws six inches more water than the Northerner.

SICK HORSES.

The horses do not appear to stand hardships and privations as well as the men. On short feed, condensed sea water, with no exercise, they grow sick and debilitated. A schooner is lying but a short distance from us, with a deck-load of horses, belonging to a Rhode Island battery, and they are jumping them overboard, and swimming them ashore. It is curious to observe the horses as they are led up to the gangway; to see them brace themselves back and shudder to take the fearful leap. But a little encouragement from half a dozen men in their rear pushing them, over they go, and as they come up out of the water, they shake their heads and snort, and put for the nearest land, where they are rubbed dry, blanketed and led off up the island.

ACROSS THE SWASH.

The Northerner has crossed into the sound, and anchored: As she got off and moved into the sound, cheer after cheer went up from all the fleet, the bands playing and all having a big time generally.

JAN. 26. Quite a number of boats have been hauled off, and are now lying in the sound. They are still at work on the Eastern Queen, which seems to be as firmly imbedded in the sand as were her timbers in the soil in which they grew. The steamer Louisiana, with the 6th New Hampshire aboard, lies high and dry on the shoal, and it will be a job to get her off, but I reckon she will have to come, or come to pieces. When half a dozen big steamers get hold they make a pretty strong team, and something has got to come or break. I learn she is hogged, whatever that is. I shouldn't be surprised if she was, if she has been well supplied with this gull bait they call pork.

We had religious services this morning and afternoon, the first we have had since leaving Annapolis. We had excellent singing, and the chaplain's remarks were well timed and to the point. He recounted the dangers and troubles, which under the blessing of God, we have been brought through, and spoke words of cheer and comfort for the future.

THE CURLEW.

JAN. 27. Preparations are going on this morning to get the New York across the bar. We were transferred to the steam ferry-boat Curlew, and are now anchored in the sound. The New York is to be lightened of everything on board, and it is thought, with a full sea and some help, she may be able to cross. We are in the most disagreeable and uncomfortable quarters we have yet been in. Every change seems to bring some new hardship, and with a few more changes for the worse we shall be able to learn how great are our powers of endurance. We are packed in here as thick as bees with scarcely standing room, and the old craft is open at both ends, admitting the cold winds and rains, besides being as wet and dirty as a stable. If it should rain hard enough to drive us in from the ends of the boat and from off the deck, a part of us would have to lie down in our bunks to give standing room for the rest. I should think the water casks were a cemetery for dead rats by the way the water tastes; condensed sea water is a luxury to it, and byway of encouragement we are told that we are to have some tomorrow. There are, however, a few casks of good water aboard, but we are not allowed any of it. I reckon the boys will manage to get some of it. If they don't, it will be an exception to their general smartness. The officers and

MY DIARY.   29

crew of the old hulk are cross and crabbed, and unless they alter their tactics, I fear they will get enough of us before we have been here many days.

A STRANGER.

JAN. 28. Work is still going on, getting the boats off and getting them across the bar. The Eastern Queen is afloat and will be with us today. The little steamer Pilot Boy, with Generals Burnside and Foster aboard, is flying around among the vessels of the fleet, giving orders to the boat commanders and commanders of troops. The sutler came aboard today; he is quite a stranger and the boys gathered around him, asking him a thousand questions. He brought with him a small stock of fruit and other notions which went off like hot cakes at any price which he chose to ask. Some of the boys thought the prices pretty high, but they should consider that it is with great difficulty and expense that things are got here at all. They have the advantage, however, in not being obliged to buy, if they think the charges too much. The Eastern Queen is coming across the swash, the bands are all playing and cheers are going out from all the fleet.

THE SIGNAL CORPS ARRIVES.

JAN. 29. The long lost signal corps arrived today. We gave them a great ovation; flags and streamers flying, bands playing and cheering from all the boats. They have had ahard time of it, having been fourteen days on the passage from Fortress Monroe. They ran out to sea in the first great storm, and the succession of storms has prevented them from getting in. They were well nigh famished when they arrived.

GOOD WATER.

We are today luxuriating on good water, the first we have had for many days. Some of the boys last night got in the rear of the forbidden water casks, and by a vigorous use of a jack-knife, succeeded in tapping a cask. Any quantity of canteens (mine among the rest), were filled with the contraband water, and if the thing is kept still today there will be a big haul tonight. Our fare is pretty short, and of a kind never dreamed of in the cabin of a first-class ocean steamer. Still it answers to keep us breathing, and perhaps that is as much as we can expect while on this excursion. We are thriving on a half ration of steamed pork and hardtack, with condensed sea water. The half ration of pork is a bountiful supply; it is so strong and oily a very little answers the purpose, and hardtack is the chief dependence. But for water, we shall do well enough so long as we can steal it. Coffee is entirely out of the question, for on this craft there is no chance for the cooks to make it in great quantities, although they do manage to make a small amount for the officers. None of us are allowed down in the fireroom, so that shuts us off from making coffee or scouse.

I suggested to a few of the faithful the plan of getting down on the bottom of the boat, under the boilers, and kindling a fire there and making some. They seemed to think that it would be rather a desperate undertaking, besides they would smoke themselves out before they had half accomplished their purpose.

JAN. 30. Our canteens are again filled with the contraband water, so we shall be all right today as far as that is concerned. Some of the boys made a raid last night on the sutler's stuff and appropriated to themselves pretty much what he had. I cannot approve of that, as the sutler is at a good deal of trouble and expense to get a few notions for us and probably sells them as cheap as he can afford. The boys ought not to steal from him, at this time especially, as there are those who would be glad to buy. A schooner came down today to take a look at us, one of our boats gave chase, but a good breeze blowing, the schooner had the advantage and got away. This afternoon a small boat was seen coming down flying a white flag. The boat contained one darkey who had risked the perils of the sound to escape from the land of Jeff, the house of bondage.

A DISCOVERY.

A great discovery has just been made and isn't there larks now, though. The skipper is foaming with rage. An account of stock has been taken, and a cask or two of water is missing. On inspection it was found tapped at the wrong end. A very mysterious circumstance, but such things are liable to happen. A strong guard has been placed over the other casks.

JAN. 31. This morning a small schooner was seen coming down the sound. A boat went out and met her; she contained seven darkies who said they stole the schooner and left in her from Roanoke island. They were put aboard the steamer S. R. Spaulding, and the little schooner hitched astern. They can probably give some valuable information in regard to affairs on the island. The New York is stuck on the swash, and several boats and tugs are trying to pull her across; she will probably get off tomorrow. They will then all be across, except the Louisiana, which will be here in a day or two. We got a big mail today; any quantity of letters and newspapers, and the boys are cheered up wonderfully to hear from home.

A RAIN STORM.

FEB. 1. A very heavy rain set in last night and continued until 9 o'clock this morning. The old Curlew looks as though she had been down cruising for mermaids and came back disappointed. She is all afloat, fore, aft and amidships; the rain drove in at the ends, the deck leaked and altogether we had a pretty rough night of it. I cannot say how the others slept, but my sleep was anything but balmy. I did not, in fact, dream of dwelling in marble halls.

The New York has crossed the bar and we are again aboard

of her; thank our lucky stars. Good-bye, old Curlew! and may you find a sweet and lasting repose at the bottom of the sound before you are many days older. Our bill of fare this week consisted of steamed pork and hardtack of a poor quality, and short supply at that. Since they caught us stealing water, the fluid has been the meanest kind of condensed sea water, the poorest we have yet had.

Feb. 2. A high wind prevailed this morning and the sea was somewhat rough; the boat had considerable motion, but the boys had their sea legs on, so it caused them very little trouble.

HIGH LIVING.

Our company cooks, with commendable enterprise and industry and with an eye to our present well being, furnished us with baked beans and hot coffee for breakfast. This was a great treat, and every man had all he wanted; a vote of thanks was given the cooks. For dinner boiled beef was served, the first we have had since leaving Fortress Monroe.

I hope this kind of fare will hold out, but fear we shall have a relapse of the worst kind. The chaplain held services in the saloon this morning and afternoon. The boys spent most of the day writing letters, reading newspapers and making up their diaries.

A GALA DAY.

Feb. 3. The winds have ceased, and the sea is as calm as an honest man's conscience. Companies are parading the decks of the steamers, a dozen bands are out playing, everybody is feeling good, and altogether, we are having quite an enlivening scene. Business is brisk today; all the boats are in the sound, and schooners are alongside of them, supplying them with coal, water and rations, preparatory to a trip up the sound. Everything now seems to be nearly ready, and I expect that some fine morning we will make a call on our southern friends. No doubt they will be delighted to see us, and as they say, to welcome us with bloody hands to hospitable graves; but perhaps it has never occurred to them that in a reception of that kind, they, perchance, may fill some of the aforesaid graves. I had much rather they would welcome us to a good dinner of fishballs than cannon balls; but I suppose they will have their own choice of reception and we must reciprocate the best we can.

Merchandise brings a right smart price in this market, and a man needs a heavy purse to purchase very extensively. I paid $1 for the same quantity of tobacco I bought at home for forty cents.

THE EXPEDITION MOVES.

Feb. 5. The clink of the windlass is heard on all the boats, hoisting up their anchors, so here we go for a trip up the sound, probably for Roanoke island. This island holds the Albemarle sound and all that part of North Carolina lying on it, and also

Southeast Virginia. It is quite an important point, and we learn is strongly fortified. Our fleet consists of about seventy sail of all kinds and makes an imposing appearance. The gunboats, under command of Commodore Goldsborough, take the advance, the transports and other craft following. After a few hours' sail, the low, pine-covered shore of the old North state presented itself to view. We were in sight of the shore all day and not a house was to be seen or any visible signs of life, excepting huge columns of smoke rising above the tree-tops. These were probably signal fires, as they could be seen along the shore as far as the eye could reach. We sailed today to within ten miles of the light-house at the western end of the Pamlico sound, the entrance to Croatan sound, in which is situated the coveted island. Here we dropped anchor for the night, the gunboats forming a picket guard, and extending themselves nearly to the light-house. The island can be seen through a glass, and tomorrow I expect we shall get a nearer view.

FEB. 6. Hoisted anchor and steamed to within a short distance of the light house, and in full view of the island. Here we again dropped anchor and the day was spent in prospecting by the gunboats. They went up near the island, and after a few hours returned, reporting three forts and a number of armed boats and schooners. The thing is being managed pretty cautiously, and I expect when the show comes off, it will be ahead of anything we ever saw, not excepting Barnum's. For one, I am not over anxious to see a fight, and especially to be a participant, but we have been afloat so long and fared so hard I wish to get ashore, no matter under what circumstances. One would have supposed, to have heard the boys talk last night, that we were all Napoleons. They talked of booming guns, the rattle of infantry, of splendid bayonet charges, brilliant victories, and deeds of courage, daring and heroism. On the principle, I suppose of those who know nothing fear nothing, but then it is a good plan not to get our tails down until we are obliged to. I even got my courage screwed up so I could repeat the words of some great military hero or other:

> "Then welcome war, our arms to brace,
> The standards planted face to face;
> Tho' death's pale horse leads on the chase,
>   We'll follow there."

Ammunition was dealt out today, and our cartridge boxes now contain forty rounds of the death-dealing missiles. The boys seem to be in great spirits and the bands are discoursing national music.

THE BOMBARDMENT.

FEB. 7. A thick fog prevailed this morning and continued until about 9 o'clock, when it lifted and the gunboats got under way. Slowly they steamed towards the island and took their positions before the forts, but at a sufficient distance not to incur much damage from them. We were all eagerly watching the movements of the boats, when at about 10 o'clock, we saw a white cloud rise from one of the boats, and the next moment a huge column of dirt and sand rose from the enemy's works, showing the effect of the shot. The fort replied from all its guns, but their shots fell short as the boats lay beyond their range. The bombardment now commenced in earnest, the boats sailing in a circle, and delivering their fire as they passed the fort. Their firing was not rapid, but well directed. The fort's guns blazed away as rapidly as possible, doing some damage to the boats. At noon the transports commenced the passage of the narrow channel into Croatan sound. From here we had a much nearer and better view of the bombardment. The boats were sailing much nearer the fort and firing more rapidly. They had driven the men from the guns on the fort, and their fire was feebly replied to. At this time the shells from the boats had set the barracks and other buildings near the fort on fire. Great clouds of smoke and flame rose from the burning buildings, and the boats belched forth their fire more furiously than ever, the shots tearing up the parapet of the fort or burying themselves in the mound of sand covering the magazine. It was truly a grand and fearful exhibition! Thousands looked on with breathless suspense, expecting every moment to see the magazine blow up or the rebels strike their colors.

The enemy's gunboats, which had been idle spectators behind the blockade, now came to the rescue; but a few well directed shots from 100-pounder rifles sent them reeling back to their places. From this time the boats had things their own way, the fort occasionally firing a shot as much as to say, we never surrender. During the bombardment a small sloop or yacht attracted a good deal of attention. She carried one 100-pounder gun. She lay low in the water, below the range of the enemy's guns, and was skilfully handled. She sailed in the circle, running close up to the fort and delivering her fire with telling effect. With every shot she fired she was cheered by the fleet; all the bands playing.

THE LANDING.

About 2 p. m., preparations were made to land the troops. The little steamer Pilot Boy, with Gen. Foster aboard, and about half a mile of barges in tow, was seen approaching our boat. I was standing near Col. Upton, at the gangway forward the wheelhouse, as the Pilot Boy ran alongside, and heard Gen. Foster tell the colonel to order his men to load with ball cartridge, take three days' rations and come aboard his boat and the barges as soon as possible. This loading with ball cartridge was a new order to me; it implied that our holiday soldiering was over. A peculiar feeling such as I had never before experienced came over me; I felt it to the very taps of my brogans, and thought I would rather be excused. I turned around and without saying a word to anyone went down stairs. Drawing Spitfire from its hiding place, I dropped in the little messenger that if needs be perhaps might carry mourning and sorrow to some southern hearthstone. In quick time we left the New York and were going towards the shore, followed by other boats containing the balance of our brigade. The intention was to land about four miles above the fort, in a little nook called Ashby bay, near Ashby house; but as we neared the bay, a line of bayonets seen above the bushes, going double quick in that direction, changed the general's mind, and we turned our course towards a marsh a mile or more nearer the fort. As we ran alongside the marsh where we were to land, Captain Pickett of company A made a leap for the land, going half way to his neck in mud and water. He was the first man on the island. At this time the line of bayonets above the bushes was seen coming back. The little gunboat Delaware now came up and commenced shelling the bushes and woods to cover our landing. In a few minutes we were all on the marsh and wading through the mud and water for the hard land, a distance of some forty rods. On reaching this we soon came out to a small clearing, on which was a house, barn and out-buildings, the occupants of which had suddenly taken their leave. Here we found things as the occupants had left them, the cat quietly sitting in the corner and the tea-kettle singing over the fire.

Adjutant Harkness and Lieutenant Richter of company G climbed to the top of the house and nailed thereon a small flag in honor, I suppose, of our landing and notice of our intention of staying. Company A, Capt. Pickett, and company K, Capt. Denny, were sent out on a reconnoissance. They soon returned, reporting no enemy near.

5 p. m. Foster's brigade had all landed, and by dark nearly the whole division were ashore. Now commenced the work of carrying rails and planks to build a road across the marsh to get the howitzers of the marine artillery ashore. Soon after dark, Gen. Foster, with the 21st Massachusetts and a section of the marine artillery, hauling their howitzers, went past us into the woods to establish his picket line. After a while the general returned, and said we might build fires and make ourselves comfortable. Fires were kindled and we began to look around for places to sleep, but a rain setting in, put an end to that. In the rain we stood around the camp-fires through the long night, while an occasional shot out in the woods served to keep up a little excitement and prevent us from getting sleepy.

BATTLE OF ROANOKE ISLAND.

FEB. 8. At daylight, the order to fall in was heard on all sides. Putting on my equipments and taking Spitfire and a big sweet potato, which I had with much labor succeeded in baking, I took my place in my company. The brigade all ready, Gen. Foster gave the order to march. He, with Col. Upton, took his place at the right of our regiment, marching by the flank into the woods. We soon came out to the pickets and the road that runs through the island. Here we filed to the left, marching up the road. Company A, Capt. Pickett, was thrown out as skirmishers. They soon fell in with the enemy's pickets and drove them in. The column moved up the road to within a short distance of the clearing, in front of the rebel works. On the right of the road the ground was hard and free from brush, but on the left was an almost impenetrable swamp, covered with a dense growth of tangle-brush and horse briars. The right wing of the regiment filed to the right, while the left plunged into the swamp, and with swords and jack-knives, succeeded in cutting a path until they had penetrated the swamp far enough to form our line. The regiment was now nearly all in the swamp, the right resting just across the road. The howitzer battery had taken position in the road, in front of our right wing. The 23d and 27th Massachusetts formed on our right, while the 10th Connecticut was held in reserve. We were now in line in the swamp, and facing to the front, commenced firing. The battery had already opened the ball, and were receiving the attention of the enemy in front.

We could see nothing to shoot at, but taking our range by the smoke of the enemy's guns we blazed away. We fired high, low and obliquely, thinking if we covered a wide range of ground, we might possibly lame somebody, and it seemed our shots must have proved troublesome, for they turned their attention to us, pouring musketry and canister shot without stint into the swamp. We were up to our knees in mud and water, so their shot passed over us without doing much damage. We were now ordered to cease firing and advance, but how to advance was the question. We could stand on a bog and cut away the briars in front of us and jump to another one; where they were not too large we could crawl through them, tearing not only our clothes but our hides as well. The officers rendered good service in cutting away the briars with their swords. In this way we could advance a few steps at a time and then fire a few rounds; the enemy all this time showing us marked attention.

Capt. Foster of company D was the first man I saw hit. I was watching him as he stood on a bog, cutting away the briars with his sword, and thinking of him as colonel of the old 8th regiment Massachusetts volunteer militia, in which I used to muster. The shot struck him near the eye. He whirled round on the bog, and would have fallen had not three of his men caught him and led him to the rear.

I was rather amused at the major's plan of rifle practice; he was practicing with a large revolver, shooting into the air at an elevation of about 80 degrees. Some one asked him what he was trying to act out. "Why," replied the major, "you see my shots attain their summit directly over the enemy, and if one of those shot in falling should hit a man on top of his head, his goose is cooked just as effectually as though he had been hit with a cannon ball."

By cutting and crowding ourselves through the briars, we advanced to within about 300 yards of the enemy. Our ammunition being now exhausted and having been in the swamp about three hours we were ordered out. The 21st Massachusetts took our places and the 51st New York and 51st Pennsylvania regiments forced their way through to the left front; the three regiments succeeded in getting out on the enemy's right flank. Seeing that all was now lost, the rebels took to their heels for the head of the island, followed by Reno's and Foster's brigades. At the head of the island, near the enemy's camp, was Gen. Burnside with the 24th Massachusetts regiment, to whom Col. Shaw, in command of the Confederate forces, surrendered. By this, about 3000 prisoners, with their arms, ammunition and stores, fell into our hands. But the greatest prize of all, old ex-Governor Wise, slipped through our fingers. Perhaps, having some premonitions of the fate which awaited his command, he wisely took himself off the island last night, leaving his command with Col. Shaw, of the 8th North Carolina regiment. The old governor probably acted on the principle of the militia captain who was about leading his company into action. He made them a little speech, telling them to be brave and valiant, not to run until actually forced to. "But," he said, "in case that should happen, and I being a little lame, I think I had better start now."

THOUGHTS.

During the action I had seen quite a number hit and led back to the rear, but I had little time to think much about it. After the chase commenced and we marched through the little redoubt and over the ground held by the enemy, and I began to see the mangled forms of dead and dying men, I was filled with an indescribable horror and wanted to go right home. I now began to realize what we had been doing, and thought that, if in this age of the world, with all our boasted civilization and education, men could not settle their differences short of cutting each other's throats, we were not very far removed from barbarism. But I suppose so long as the nature of man is ambitious and selfish he will try to obtain by force what he cannot attain by other means. It was about night when we reached the Confederate camp, found the business had all been done, and Gen. Burnside was master of the situation. We now appropriated to our own use the log barracks of the enemy, leaving them to secure lodgings as best they could, as we had done the night before, with only this difference; they had a large body-guard over them, to see that they were orderly and kept the peace.

MY DIARY.

AFTER THE BATTLE.

FEB. 9. A hard looking lot this morning, and no doubt feeling as hard as we looked. Tired, hungry, ragged, covered with mud, and sore from our flesh being torn and scratched with the tangle-brush and briars through which we forced ourselves yesterday. After a good ration of whiskey and a breakfast of fried bacon, with hot coffee, we began to limber up and feel a little more natural. We can now look over the field and see the results of yesterday's work. Our regiment lost six killed and 47 wounded, some of them probably fatally. Our whole loss was 42 killed and 209 wounded. The enemy's loss is not known, but is probably less than ours. Today the gunboats are after the Confederate flotilla and no doubt will give them a taste of what happened yesterday. It will probably be reported at headquarters in Richmond that their navy in these waters has become a thing of the past. Our march up from the battle-ground, yesterday afternoon, was rather an interesting one, if men nearly dying from exhaustion can be said to get interested. The trees for a mile in front of our line are marked and scarred by our shot, showing the terrible effectiveness of our rifles. The road was strewn with guns, knapsacks, equipments, blankets and everything that impeded their retreat or which they thought they had no further use for. Passing a little brown house by the wayside I noticed quite a crowd of surgeons and officers standing around. Crowding my way up to the little open window, I saw the pale, quivering form of a young man lying on a cot, with a slight covering over him, apparently in a dying condition. I inquired if any one knew who he was, and was told it was Capt. O. Jennings Wise, son of ex-Governor Wise. He had received a mortal wound and could not possibly survive many minutes. He was editor of one of the Richmond papers and captain of the Richmond Light Infantry Blues, the crack company of that city. He was a brave young fellow, and his was the last company to leave the redoubt, and then only when he fell mortally wounded.

THE PRISONERS.

FEB. 10. The prisoners are a motley looking set, all clothed (I can hardly say uniformed) in a dirty looking homespun gray cloth. I should think every man's suit was cut from a design of his own. Some wore what was probably meant for a frock coat, others wore jackets or roundabouts; some of the coats were long skirted, others short; some tight fitting, others loose; and no two men were dressed alike. Their head covering was in unison with the rest of their rig; of all kinds, from stovepipe hats to coonskin caps; with everything for blankets, from old bedquilts, cotton bagging, strips of carpet to Buffalo robes. The Wise legion are a more soldierly looking set; they wear gray cloth caps of the same pattern, and long sheep's gray overcoats with capes. Most of the officers are smart, good looking young men, wearing well-fitting gray uniforms, not unlike those of our own officers.

It is not dress altogether that makes the man or the soldier. I find among these chaps some pretty good fellows. I came across one young man from Richmond; he was smart appearing and very loquacious. In some talk I had with him he said: "This has turned out not as I wished, but not different from what I expected when we saw the force you had. In fact we had no business staying here after seeing your strength. We have met the enemy and we are theirs. I accept the situation and am glad it is no worse. I am Secesh clear through, and after I am exchanged, shall be at you again. We are now enemies, but in peace friends, and when this little dispute is settled, if any of you fellows ever come to Richmond, hunt me up. If alive, you will be welcome as long as you choose to stay, and when you leave, if you don't say you have had as right smart a time as you ever had, call me a liar and I will call you gentlemen." The fellow gave me his card and said his father owned a plantation just out of the city.

I met one fellow, a long, lank, lean, long-haired, sullen, cadaverous looking chap, and asked him what he was doing here. "Well," he said, "not much; but you 'uns was right smart to get through that swamp. We thought the devil couldn't get through it." "So you think what the devil can't do, Yankees can't, do you? You mustn't take the devil for your guage in estimating Yankees; if you do you will always get beat. We can give him points, and beat him every time." He looked a little incredulous, but did not seem inclined to go into any argument about it.

These fellows threw away a good many pistols and knives which they carried, many of which our boys have found. The knives are large, coarse, ugly looking things, forged at some country blacksmith shop, by a bungling workman, out of old rasps, scythe-points and anything containing steel. I asked one fellow what they carried those knives for, what use they put them to? "Oh!" he said, "them's Yankee slayers." "Yankee slayers? And have you slain many Yankees with them?" "Wal, no, but we thought they mought come handy in close action." "And did you think you would ever get near enough to the Yankees to use them?" "Wal, we didn't know but we mought." "Well, sir, those knives are too heavy to carry, and you don't need to carry them, for long before you would ever get near enough to the Yankees to use them the places that now know you would know you no more forever."

The boys are mixing in among the prisoners, talking over the fight, trading jack-knives, buttons and such small notions as they happen to have, and getting acquainted with each other. The weather is warm and pleasant, like May. The robins and other birds are singing as in summer. The robins seem like old friends and neighbors and I cannot help thinking that perhaps some of

MY DIARY.   39

them had their nests last summer in the trees and bushes which grow in our own dooryards and gardens at home.

Our gunboats have wiped from the face of the earth that part of the Confederate navy which prowled around these waters. They chased them up the Pasquotank river to Elizabeth City, where, after less than an hour's engagement, the enemy set their boats on fire and fled.

SETTLING PROPERTY TITLES.

FEB. 12. The Confederate officers have been paroled and sent to Elizabeth City, up the Pasquotank river. The 25th had the distinguished *honor* of escorting them and carrying a part of their baggage to the wharf where they took the boat. I reckon it must have been rather pleasing to those officers to see Yankee soldiers taking their luggage for them, but this disgrace must have been a thoughtless mistake on the part of the colonel or whoever ordered it. Those officers had with them their colored servants, but after they were all captured, officers and servants were a good deal mixed as to who they belonged to. When the officers were about leaving, Gen. Burnside settled the question. He told the darkies they could decide for themselves; they could go with their masters or stop here, just as they liked. A few of them went with their masters, the rest staid back to take their chances with the Yankees.

PAROLING THE PRISONERS.

FEB. 18. The prisoners are all paroled, and were sent off to-day. Paroling the prisoners was rather interesting to the lookers on. They were required to affix their autographs to the parole, and it was curious to observe that a large majority of them wrote it the same way, simply making the letter X. Capt. Messenger, the provost marshal, was master of ceremonies. He is a very eccentric man, and many of the prisoners scarcely knew whether to be pleased or frightened at the curious questions he asked and remarks he made to them.

HISTORY.

FEB. 23. The boys are amusing themselves making pipes from briar roots and fixing long stems of cane to them. Some of them are carved very handsomely and show much artistic skill. Washington's birthday was celebrated by salutes from the forts and a holiday in the camp. There is some very interesting history connected with this island, but not having books to refer to, I can give but a very indifferent account of it. Sometime in the latter part of the 16th century, Sir Walter Raleigh, an English nobleman, sent out an American exploring expedition. They visited the Pamlico and Albemarle sounds, discovering this island. After trading with the Indians, and learning what they could of the country, they returned to England. They gave such glowing accounts of the country and what they had seen that Raleigh, the next year, sent out a colony under one Lane. They occupied this island, but after about a year, during which time they suffered many hardships, returned to England. A year or two later, another expedition was sent out. They also settled here, but after a while the leader of it returned to England for supplies. After an absence of a year or two, he again returned here, but on landing, not a trace of it could be found, and it was never after heard from. A later historian, however, says the Indians who lived on the island claimed that some of their ancestors were white people and could talk out of a book.

HUNTING FOR RELICS.

FEB. 25. This being a warm, sunny day, a small party of us thought we would take a stroll up to the head of the island, a mile or two, and perhaps we might find some traces or relics of Raleigh's expedition. Arriving at our destination, we discovered a large, weather-beaten two-storied house, built at some remote period, and surrounded by large live oak trees. We had not the slightest doubt but that this was the house built by Lane and his party. Seeing a man standing outside, whom we supposed was the gentlemanly proprietor of the ranche, we approached, and saluting him very respectfully, inquired if he was in receipt of any recent advices from Raleigh's expedition. He looked at us in utter astonishment and said he knew nothing about it and reckoned there had been "no sich expedition yere." He said, "Burnside's expedition was yere," and "reckoned that was about enough;" he couldn't see the use of any more coming. We bade the gentleman good day and left. In looking around for relics, Whipple picked up an old shoe heel. Here was a prize surely, a veritable relic of Raleigh's party. Whipple put it in his pocket. intending, as he said, to send it to the antiquarian society at Worcester, and indulging in the hope that for presenting such a priceless relic, they would at least vote him an honorary member of the society. Relics being scarce, we went up to the shore where we could look up the Albemarle. The wind was blowing gently down the sound, and the little rollers were breaking on the beach at our feet. It was pretty warm; the water looked clear and really refreshing. Some one proposed taking a dip. No sooner said than off came our clothes and in we plunged. Egad! such a scrambling and floundering to get out is seldom seen. It reminded me of a basket of lobsters turned into a tub of scalding water. The water was ice cold, and I thought I should certainly freeze before getting out. After getting on my clothes and getting warm, I certainly felt better for my bath. It was agreed by all hands that February was the wrong season of the year for out-door bathing. Whipple is despondent, his hopes are dashed. He came to me and informed me that he had carefully inspected the shoe heel, and found it put together with cut nails, which are a much more recent invention than Raleigh's expedition.

CHAPTER III.

WE LEAVE ROANOKE ISLAND.

MARCH 6. Broke camp, leaving our log barracks, and are once more aboard our old home, the New York. We were cordially welcomed by Capt. Clark, Mr. Mulligan and the crew. Mr. Mulligan said he knew we were doing our duty on the 8th of February by the racket we made and the smoke rising above the tree tops.

MARCH 9. A beautiful Sabbath morning, not a ripple disturbs the smooth surface of the sound. Religious services this morning in the saloon; in the afternoon on the promenade deck. All the troops, except one or two regiments, left to garrison the island, are again afloat, and the talk now is that Newbern is the next point of attack.

ON A SHOAL.

MARCH 11. This morning the clink of the windlass is again heard from all the boats hoisting their anchors. We steam out of Croatan into Pamlico sound; so here we go for new conquests.

> The Burnside expedition, it did not end in smoke;
> It captured Elizabeth City, and the isle of Roanoke.

About 11 a. m., the New York went on to a shoal and came to a dead halt. Here was a pretty fix, stuck right in the middle of Pamlico sound. We had the schooner Skirmisher in tow, with companies K and I aboard, but they thought they would leave us and go it alone. Accordingly they hauled in their hawser, hoisted sail and left us, sailing with a fair breeze gallantly down the sound. Three large steamers hitched on to us, to pull us off. After a good deal of hard work, lots of swearing and breaking hawsers, they finally succeeded, about 4 p. m., in hauling us off. We again started and dropped anchor at Hatteras inlet at 10 p. m.

THE START FOR NEWBERN.

MARCH 12. This morning weighed anchor and our fleet, comprising upwards of 50 sail, steamed up the Pamlico sound for Newbern. After a few hours' sail, large numbers of wild geese and ducks attracted our attention. Wide marshes which extend into the sound are their feeding ground, and from these they make their way a long distance into the sound. These waters appear to be their winter quarters. About 3 p. m., we enter the Neuse river, which is here about two miles wide. Situated on the left bank, thirty miles up the river, is the city of Newbern. Slowly we steam up the river, seeing nothing but the low, piney shores, and the smoke of the enemy's signal fires. About 8 p. m., when 15 miles up the river, in a wide place forming a kind of bay, we dropped anchor for the night. The transports lay huddled together in the middle of the river, while a cordon of gunboats surrounds us as a picket. A dark, black night has settled down on us, and all is still and silent as the tomb. Not a sound is heard or a light seen, save the enemy's signal fires, far up the river. This stillness is dreadful. It is really oppressive, and seems as though it has remained unbroken since the morning of creation. Our errand here is to make an attempt to occupy the city of Newbern, and if anybody attempts to stop us, there will be a big fight and somebody will be hurt.

THE LANDING AND MARCH.

MARCH 13. The morning of the 13th was dark and rainy, and we made preparations to land. It always rains where we go; first at Hatteras, then at Roanoke and now here. I think we are rightly named a *water* division.

We landed in a mudhole, at the mouth of Slocum's creek. Before noon the troops were all landed, and the march commenced. The 25th taking the advance, we marched up the river bank about a mile, the gun-boats shelling the woods in advance of us. We then struck into the woods, which presented a novel appearance. There was no undergrowth, but a short grass covered the ground, while masses of long gray moss hung in festoons from the branches of the trees, giving them a weird and sombre appearance. We soon came out to a cart road, or horse path, along which we followed for about a couple of miles, when we came to a deserted cavalry camp. I reckon when they heard the sounds of revelry on the river, there was mountings in hot haste, and they sped away to some safer locality. The clouds now broke and the sun shone out hot, which, together with the mud, made the march a toilsome one. A little further on, we came to the carriage road. Here Foster's brigade halted, to let Reno's and Parke's brigades move past us.

As Parke's brigade marched past us, we saw at the right of one of the companies in the 5th Rhode Island regiment, marching by the side of the orderly, a lady, dressed in a natty suit, with high boots and jockey hat, surmounted by a big ostrich feather. She was the observed of our whole brigade, and cheer after cheer went up along the line for the pretty woman. Continuing our march a little farther we reached some extensive earthworks, which were abandoned, but for what reason we of course were ignorant. But we reasoned that if they build works like these and then make no effort to hold them, it shows they are weak and have no confidence in their ability to successfully contend against us, and Newbern will fall an easy prey. The deep mud in the road, together with the heat, began to tell on the boys, and many of them were obliged to fall out by the way. Our march began to grow slower, and when about dusk, it commenced raining again, we turned into the woods at the right of the road, where we were to bivouac for the night. Scouting parties and pickets were sent out in order to give notice if anything unusual was about to transpire during the night. Here in the soft mud of the swamp, with the rain pouring down on us, was our hotel. Mrs. Hemans, in her song of the Pilgrims, said,

"Amidst the storm they sang."

But there was no song in that swamp; too tired for supper the boys laid themselves down in the mud to sleep, and bitterly thought of the morrow. Stokes and I roomed together between a couple of logs. Taking our rifles and powder between us and covering ourselves closely in the blankets, we were soon fast asleep. But he kept the advantage of me all night, for he is a great fellow to pull blankets, and he came out in the morning all right and dry, while I had been catching the rain. The boys slept well, but woke up cold and wet. There was no time to make a cup of coffee, for we were close on the enemy, and the order was again to the battle. We caught a few hasty mouthfuls of cold meat and hardtack, and quietly fell into our places in line.

THE BATTLE.

We fellows who do the shooting are not counted as any great shakes ordinarily, but yesterday morning we seemed to be regarded as of very great importance, and it took a great amount of swearing and hurrying to and fro of aids and hoarse shoutings of officers to get us around where we were wanted. We were within a half mile of the enemy's line, and Reno's and Parke's brigades were deploying in front of them, on the centre and left of our line. Foster's brigade was to take the right, and the 25th led off up the road, followed by the 24th Massachusetts and the other regiments of the brigade. We soon came in sight of the enemy's works, which were only a short rifle-shot from us. Reno's and Parke's brigades had already opened the ball along the center and left. We filed out of the road to the right, moving towards the river. As we moved out we were honored with a salute from one of the enemy's batteries, but the shots passed harmlessly over our heads. The boys looked a little wild, but with steady step moved on until the 25th and 24th Massachusetts were in line on the right of the road; the 27th and 23d Massachusetts and the 10th Connecticut regiments were on the left.

Foster's brigade was now in line of battle and moving forward towards the edge of the woods next to the clearing. The howitzer battery now came up, took position in the road, between the 24th and 27th Massachusetts, and commenced firing. With the exception of the 25th, Foster's brigade then opened fire. We were on the extreme right and well towards the river, seeing nothing in front of us to draw our fire. The 24th Massachusetts kept up a scattering fire that kept the enemy well down behind their works.

We were ordered, if possible, to turn the enemy's left. We

advanced nearly to the edge of the woods, and only a short distance from the enemy's line. I was running my eye along it to see where and how it ended, expecting every moment to hear the order to charge, but just then the boats commenced throwing shell over us, towards the Confederate line. They had got a low range and their shells were coming dangerously near, splintering and cutting off the trees, and ploughing great furrows in the ground directly in front of us. In this condition of affairs we were compelled to fall back. The boats, however, were soon notified of their mistake and ceased firing. We again advanced, going over and beyond from where we fell back, when all at once we received a galling flank fire from an unseen battery. We again fell back a few rods, dressing the line and again cautiously advanced. We now discovered that their works curved and connected with a large water battery, situated just in the edge of the woods and concealed by the trees. In the rear of this battery were mounted old 32-pounder marine guns, which gave them an enfilading fire of the clearing in front of their works. From these guns they fired grape shot, which weighed about four pounds each. To charge was hopeless, and in falling back we received another fire from this battery. From these we lost quite a number of men, killed and wounded. I had the honor of stopping one ball myself; it struck a tree, however, before it did me. Having got back from under the guns of this battery, Col. Upton reported the situation to Gen. Foster, who ordered him to move his regiment to the left of the 24th Massachusetts and support the howitzer battery.

During all this time, however, the battle was raging furiously along the centre and left. While we were bothering around on the right, a little incident occurred, which perhaps is worthy of mention. Lieut. Draper of my company (B), but now attached to the signal corps, reported to Capt. Clark for duty. He said there was nothing more for the signal corps to do and he would like to take his place in the line. The captain told him he could do as he liked; he thereupon joined his company, and did duty with it the rest of the day. Although a young man of only 20 years of age, he has got the stuff in him of which soldiers are made.

In front of our battery the enemy had a large gun which commanded the road, and which proved rather troublesome. This gun after each discharge was hauled around, and again back into position, by a pair of mules. After each discharge a young dare-devil of a marine lieutenant would run down the road almost to the gun, to see what they were up to. On one of these excursions he discovered one of the mules down, probably from a stray shot. He came running back up the road like a wild man, swinging his cap, and shouting at the top of his voice: "Come on, come on! for God's sake, come on. Now is your time!"

The 25th, without any other order, sprang forward, followed by the 24th Massachusetts and all the line. On the charge they received a heavy fire from the enfilading battery, but on they went, scaling the ditch and parapet like blackbirds, but no enemy was there. Seeing us coming, they took that as a notice to leave, and acted on it immediately. Inside the works, I heard Gen. Burnside ask Gen. Foster who gave the order to charge. Foster replied he didn't know, but it made no difference so long as it was done.

The 25th reformed, and, marching a short distance to the rear, charged across the railroad, into the swamp, capturing Col. Avery and his South Carolina regiment, who were covering the retreat. Thus, after five hours' hard fighting, ended the battle of Newbern. Victory had again perched upon our banners, and the cheers of the victors were ringing out on every side. Although the battle resulted as I wished, I certainly did not feel like glorying for who can compute the woe, anguish and sorrow of this day's work? I cannot get over my horror of a battle,

"Where the death angel flaps his broad wing o'er the field,
And human souls go out in agony."

OUR ENTRANCE INTO NEWBERN.

Foster's brigade starts up the railroad for town, leaving Reno's and Parke's brigades to take care of the field. Cautiously we moved along, thinking, perhaps, the enemy may have formed a second line and are awaiting our approach. It soon became apparent, however, that they were making the distance between them and us as long as possible. We then hurried along, arriving at the river where the railroad bridge was burned which crossed into town. The view from here was an appalling one. The railroad bridge, a fine structure upwards of 1500 feet in length, was in ruins and the town was on fire in several places. Dense clouds of smoke of inky blackness settled like a pall over the town, while every few moments the lurid flames, with their forked tongues, would leap above the clouds, and the bellowing of the gunboats on the river, throwing their large shells over the town after the retreating enemy, conspired to make a most hideous scene.

It was near the middle of the afternoon when the old ferry boat Curlew (which a few weeks before I had wished sunk) arrived. On board this, Major McCafferty, with a mixed company of about 100 men, with the colors, crossed the river and landed on the wharf at the foot of Craven street. These were the first troops and colors in the city. After landing we marched up Craven nearly to Pollock street, when we halted. The major did not appear to have any business on hand or instructions to make any, so we waited for further orders or for the regiment to join us.

Here was presented an indescribable scene. A town on fire, an invading army entering its gates, the terror-stricken inhabitants fleeing in every direction. The negroes were holding a grand jubilee, some of them praying and in their rude way thanking God for their deliverance; others, in their wild delight, were dancing and singing, while others, with an eye to the main chance, were pillaging the stores and dwellings. But in the midst of all this appalling tumult and confusion, the boys, true to the natural instincts of the soldier, were looking around to see what could be found in the line of trophies and fresh rations. They soon began to come in with their plunder, which the major told them to carry back, as he should allow no pillaging while he was in command. Presently Stokes comes along bringing a little package. The major asked, "What have you there?" "Sausages, sir!" "Go, carry them back where you got them from." "I reckon not," replied Stokes, "a lady out here gave them to me." The major was incredulous, but Stokes offered to show him the lady and let her tell it, whereupon the former subsides, and Stokes, with a roguish twinkle of his eye, jams the package into my haversack, saying, "Sausage for breakfast." I was proud of the boy, to see how well he was observing instructions, as I have told him from the start that to stand any sort of a chance as a soldier, he must learn to do a right smart job of stealing, and be able to lie the hair right off a man's head. He has certainly shown some smartness, and I doubt if a commissioned officer could have done any better.

The regiment landed at the north side of the city, and about night rejoined us. Our hard day's work was at last finished, the regiment was dismissed and the companies quartered in any unoccupied buildings they might find. Generals Burnside and Foster, with soldiers, citizens and negroes, were putting out the fires and bringing order out of confusion. Company B was quartered in a small house on Craven street, and the boys, although hungry, tired and worn down by the fatigues of the day, made frolic of the evening and celebrated their victory.

MARCH 15. The boys came out this morning, looking a little the worse for wear, lame, sore and stiff; but with a good bumper of whiskey to lubricate their stiffened joints, and a little stirring around to take the kinks out of their legs, a good breakfast, hot coffee, etc., they soon resumed their normal condition. There is not much doing today except lying around in quarters or looking over the town. Negroes are coming in by the hundred, and the city is full of soldiers and marines traveling about and having things pretty much their own way. Guards are sent out to patrol the streets and assist Capt. Dan, the provost marshal, in preserving order preparatory to putting on a provost guard and bringing the city under law and order. Some enterprising party has hoisted the old flag on the spire of the church on Pollock street. There let it proudly wave; let it catch the first beams of the morning, and let the last rays of the setting sun linger and play amid its folds; let it gladden the hearts of every lover of liberty and loyalty, and let it be a notice to these deluded and ill-advised people around here, that it will never again give place to their traitorous rag of secession.

WE ATTEND CHURCH.

MARCH 16. Today, for the first time since we left home, Chaplain James held services in a meeting-house. We occupied the large house of the Presbyterian society, which was well filled with a miscellaneous congregation of soldiers, sailors, citizens and negroes, both men and women. Col. Upton had improvised a choir, and, with the aid of the organ, led the singing. The chaplain preached a very good discourse, and I hardly knew which felt the best, he or the colonel. There are several other meeting-houses here, which are or have been occupied by the Methodist, Baptist, Episcopalian, Catholic and negro societies. It would seem that this people have sometime been a God-fearing people, but since Jeff. Davis inaugurated a new regime, every man has done that which seemed good in his own sight. Hence we are here on this little excursion.

NEW QUARTERS.

MARCH 17. It would seem that the people had no thought of evacuating the city until the very last moment. When they saw that the Philistines were upon them they hastily gathered up their valuables and what light articles they could carry on their persons, and fled, leaving their houses, stores and property, just as they stood.

Today the several companies of our regiment moved into the deserted mansions of the Confederate martyrs, which will be our quarters during our stay. Company B went into a two-story brick house on East Front street. It has a pretty flower garden in front, with an orchard, vegetable garden and servants' quarters in the rear. The house is nicely furnished throughout; the floors, halls and stairs are carpeted, as are the chambers. The front parlor has upholstered furniture, center table, piano, lace curtains, ornaments, gas fixtures, etc. The back parlor is furnished similar to the front, excepting the piano. The basement contains all necessary culinary utensils. I don't see but we are pretty well fixed, but this is only one of the occasional sunny spots in a soldier's life. Some of the other companies are quartered in more pretentious and better furnished houses, on Pollock, Craven and Broad streets. We are nicely settled in the fine mansions of the lordly fugitives, who but yesterday ruled these spacious homes and paced the pictured halls. What strange infatuation, bordering on insanity, must have possessed these people, to bring this terrible calamity of war upon themselves, thus becoming voluntary exiles and strangers from their homes and property.

LOSS AND GAIN.

An account of stock has been taken, and we are now able to figure up the losses and gains in the great battle. The 25th lost four killed and sixteen wounded. The whole Federal loss was 100 killed and 498 wounded. The enemy's loss in killed and wounded is not known, but probably was not large, as they were behind their works, and all their killed and wounded were put aboard the cars which were waiting on the track. They lost about 500 men, taken prisoners, all the guns in their works, all their field batteries, upwards of 100 guns; besides all their horses, camp equipage, a large amount of ammunition, 4000 muskets and a large quantity of commissary and quartermaster's stores. They also lost three steamboats, one of which they ran ashore and burned, besides quite a quantity of cotton on the wharves which they had used in the erection of batteries.

NEWBERN.

MARCH 20. Newbern, situated at the north confluence of the Trent and Neuse rivers, was, I think, first settled by colonists from Berne, in Switzerland, and in honor of the old town was named New Berne, but for short, is now pronounced as written. The chivalry, in their hasty flight, thought to make a Moscow of it, and fired it in several places, destroying the long and expensive railroad bridge across the Trent river, all the turpentine distilleries (save one) of which there was quite a number, and three squares of the town, in one of which was the large Planter's hotel. The city has a fine water front on the south and east sides, furnishing ample wharfage for shipping and warehouses. It contains a population of about 8000. The streets cross at right angles, thus forming squares which are compactly built over. The area of the city is much less than many northern towns of 2000 inhabitants, but land is scarce here and it doesn't do to waste it for building purposes. There are, however, several fine residences with ample surroundings. There are four churches, several halls, one academy, one hotel, court house, jail, post office, printing office, and many large wholesale stores and warehouses. There is a small cotton mill, manufacturing cotton yarn, a lumber mill, one turpentine distillery, tannery, gas works, and a large machine shop and foundry connected with the railroad depot, at the north side of the city. There are two banks here, but at present they do not seem to be doing a regular banking business. Capt. Dan, the provost marshal, occupies the Merchant's, while the master of transportation occupies the bank of North Carolina. Whether the latter bank discounts or not, I am unable to say, but I know that Capt. Dan does, when there is anything in the bottle. The streets are wide and level, set on either side with handsome shade trees. Altogether it is rather a pretty city. This has been a town of some commercial importance, having had a large inland and coastwise trade, exporting shingles, staves and other lumber to the West Indies, cotton and naval stores to northern ports, and bringing return cargoes of such goods as the market here demanded.

I AM INTERVIEWED.

MARCH 21. Passing along Pollock, above Middle street, to-day, I was accosted by a man who was sitting on the veranda of his house and invited to come in, as he wished a talk with me. Noticing that he was a smart-looking, well-dressed, gentlemanly-appearing man, and withal an M. D., according to his sign, I was nothing loth to gratify his whim. As I stepped up on the veranda, he invited me to be seated. After a little commomplace talk, he began to inquire about our troops, their number and where they were from. I told him only a few of our troops had landed, that the river and sound were black with them in case they should be needed, and nearly all of them were from New England. He said our capture of the city was wholly unexpected, and at the last moment nearly all the better class of citizens left, leaving their houses and property as we found them. He said in that he thought they had made a great mistake, as he regarded Gen. Burnside as an honorable, high-toned gentleman, who would have dealt fairly with them, if they had remained and taken their chances, and would have allowed them to go whenever they wished. I replied I didn't know how that would have been, but I thought they had made another mistake in burning the railroad bridge and trying to burn the town. In doing as they have, they have shown that they had no regard for their property and they certainly cannot expect us to have much for it, although we have shown some in putting out the fires and saving it.

"Yes, I know," he said, "but perhaps they thought they would show your people that they were willing to sacrifice their property and make a Moscow of it rather than let it fall into your hands."

"Well, sir," said I, "in that they made another mistake, for if they had succeeded in burning it, it would have been no Moscow; we should have staid here just the same. Unlike Napoleon, we do not need the town; we care nothing for it; it is the position we want."

"But you seem to occupy it?"

"Certainly we do, there is no one else to occupy it, and we may as well use it as not."

"Do you propose to have us vacate our premises for your use?"

"Really, sir, I am not in the secrets of the general, but I presume that you and all others will be protected in your persons and property, so long as you remain loyal and show no opposition to the government."

"Yes, sir, I supposed it would be something that way. What do you propose doing with that cotton down on the wharf."

"That cotton belonged to the Confederate government, or at least they were using it against the Federal government, and like other government property it becomes the spoils of war, and some fine morning you will see it going down the river bound for some northern manufacturing city. After a few weeks it will be back here again in the form of tents for the use of the army."

"Then you intend making this a permanent garrison?"

"We intend to hold this position just as long as it is of any use to us."

"How long do you think this war will continue?"

"As things look now, I don't think it can possibly hold more than a year longer, if it does so long."

"Then you think in that time you can subjugate our people?"

"Well, sir, my opinion is that in less than eighteen months, every armed Confederate, unless he sooner surrenders, will be driven into the Gulf of Mexico."

"You seem to be very sanguine in your opinion, sir; but then we all have our opinions, and I think after a year you will find you have made but little progress. I would like to ask for how long you have enlisted?"

"I have enlisted for three years, unless the job is sooner finished."

"Well, sir, if nothing serious happens to you (which I really hope there will not), you will serve your three years, and then, unless your people give it up, you can again enlist, for I can assure you that our people will never give it up."

"You think then, that with all the odds against you, you will finally succeed?"

"I certainly do; you see you Yankees are going to tire of this thing after a spell; you are not used to roughing it, and will soon weary of the hardships and privations of a soldier's life. You Yankees had much rather be spinning cotton, making shoes, trading, speculating and trying to make money, than following the occupation of a soldier."

"For a choice, there are probably very few of us who would select the occupation of a soldier, but you mistake the Yankee character entirely, if you think, having undertaken anything, they tire of it very easily. That was not the class of men they sprung from. They were an enterprising, untiring class of men; if they had not been, they would never have settled down among the rocks and hills of bleak New England and made of it the richest, most intelligent and powerful little piece of territory the sun shines on. But, my friend, as all things earthly have an end, this will probably prove no exception, and in the end, your people will find that they have got the least value received for the money paid out of any speculation they ever engaged in, and will still find themselves a part and parcel of the United States, subject to all the rules and conditions of the government, in common with the rest of the states."

After some further talk about state rights and state sovereignty, in which we could not agree, he invited me into his house. Here, like a true Southern gentleman, he entertained and extended hospitalities right royally, and I think we must have sampled his best bottle. He told me it was six years old, and from a silver goblet, I sipped the best native wine I ever tasted ; it was rich, mellow and fruity. He said it was made from a choice variety of grape called the Scuppernong. It was really a splendid native wine, as so it appeared to me. After some more small talk, I bade my new found friend good day, and took my leave.

DARKIES.

MARCH 25. There are swarms of negroes here. They are of all sexes, ages, sizes and conditions. They sit along the streets and fences, staring and grinning at every thing they see, laughing and chattering together like so many black-birds. They have very exaggerated notions of freedom, thinking it means freedom from work and a license to do about as they please. There is no use trying to get them to work, for if they can get their hoe-cake and bacon, it is all they want, and they are contented and happy. When a party of them is wanted to unload a vessel or do any job of work, the commissary or quartermaster requests the colonel to send along the men. The colonel orders one of the companies to go out and pick them up and report with them where they are wanted. A patrol is detailed and put in charge of a non-commissioned officer who starts out to pick up his party. On seeing a good, stout looking fellow, the officer halts his squad, and calling the darky's attention, says, "Come here, boy!" The unsuspecting darky comes grining along up and asks, "Wat 'er want 'er me?" "Fall in here, I want you." "Wat I don' 'er want me?" "Well, I want you to do something ; fall in here," "O, lor' a gorra, boss, i'se so busy today i'se couldn't go nohow, i'se go tomorrer suah." "Never mind that, fall in here," and the darky falls in, his eyes rolling around and his thick lips sticking out, feeling about as mad as he well can, doubtless thinking that freedom is no great thing after all.

In that way the whole party is picked up in a few minutes and marched off to where they are wanted. They are set to work, and at night will all promise to be on hand the next morning, "suah." The next morning perhaps a few of them will put in an appearance, but the most of them will keep away, and another patrol will be sent out to pick up another lot. But I think, after a little while, they will learn that freedom means something besides idleness and they will feel a willingness to work. They have a curious custom of carrying everything on their heads, toting they call it, and will tote large or small bundles along the street or through a crowd as unconcernedly and safely as though it were a basket slung on their arm. They will tote a brimming pitcher or tumbler of water without spilling scarcely a drop. These darkies are a curious institution.

WE LOSE OUR MAJOR.

April 1. I learn that Major McCafferty has resigned and is going to leave us. I am sorry to learn that his ambition for fame is so soon gratified. I think a good deal of the major and shall miss him very much. He is a man of great good nature and a good deal of a humorist, and at times he makes considerable sport for the boys. The major's resignation creates a vacancy which, according to military rules will be filled by the ranking captain which is Capt. Pickett of company A. This will change the formation of the line, bringing company B on the left, and ranking second in the line. So, step by step, we ascend the ladder of fame.

LIVING HIGH.

We are now living in clover, having little else to do but to keep ourselves, clothes, arms and equipments clean and in good order. We do a little guard duty and the rest of the time is spent in reading, writing, card-playing and walking about town, seeing the fun and enjoying ourselves. Our rations are of good quality and variety. We now have our fresh beef three times a week, with all the soft bread we want. With our government rations, and what we can buy, such as oysters, fresh fish, chickens, eggs, sweet potatoes, etc., we are running at a high rate of speed. We often contrast this with our life at the inlet.

ANOTHER CHANGE IN THE LINE.

April 14. And now another change has occurred, Capt. Clark of company B has resigned. If this thing becomes chronic, I am not quite sure but I shall resign and go home, and then, perhaps, I shall be given a sutler's or horse doctor's commission and be sent back. Capt. Clark's resignation promotes First Lieut. Emery to captain, Second Lieut. Draper to first lieutenant, and first Sergeant John G. McCarter to second lieutenant. This again changes the formation of the line, and company B finds itself tenth in rank. This leaves the captain's chances for straddling a horse in the rather dim distance, but then fame, like other doubtful things, is "mighty onsartin."

BEAUTIFUL SPRING.

The vernal season is now upon us and nature is arraying herself in her most beautiful robes. The trees are in leafage, while the yards and gardens attract the eye with their almost endless variety of plants and flowers. Roses are in great variety many of them remarkable for their size and beauty, changing their hues two and three times a day. Beautiful flowering vines clamber the verandas and porticos of the houses, sending out their sweet perfume, while the air is filled with the song of birds warbling forth their happiness. This is really a charming little city, but I reckon from neglect and hard usage from the soldiers, it will soon lose its beauty. The migratory birds, such as the robin and thrush, took their leave about the middle of March. Among the birds of song that remain the mocking bird must be ranked as king. He is a noble fellow, not remarkably handsome, of a dove color, with a white spot under his wings. He is a noisy, loud-voiced fellow, an early riser, commencing his song with the first gray streaks of dawn, and he keeps up an incessant flow until about 8 o'clock, when he seeks the shade for rest and quiet. The trees are full of them, and sometimes by the noise they make one would think the trees were full of all kinds of birds. When he comes down to his fine work, one unconsciously lays aside whatever he is doing and listens with delight to his soft warble and the low trembling cadence of his sweet trills.

I GET ARRESTED.

APRIL 20. Not caring to trouble the captain all the time for passes I have got in the habit of going about town on my sagacity, and I have not yet discovered but it answers the purpose as well as a pass, but I was brought up a day or two ago, when I ran against Charley of company D, who was standing sentinel on the corner of Broad and Middle streets. I was walking leisurely along, when coming to Charley's post, he halted me and demanded my pass. I said I had not got any. He replied if that was the case it was his duty to march me to the provost's office. Rather than have any trouble with him, and to have it military in form, I handed him an old pass I happened to have in my pocket. He looked at it and tearing it up, took the position of a soldier, saying. "You non-coms are getting too big for your clothes, you are putting on altogether too many airs, but I will let you know that you can't put them on over me." I said, "Perhaps there is a shadow of truth in what you say. It is possible that they may be somewhat afflicted with inflation, but you know I am one of the meek and lowly kind." "You? You are the worst pill in the box, you never have a pass, but are all over town, in the back rooms of all the sutler's stores and taking more liberties and putting on more style than half the commissioned officers." "Now, Charley, that is a sad state of affairs indeed; but you are the first one that has found any fault with it, but if you desire the honor of escorting me to the provost's office you can have the job. After you get me there, Old Dan will give you the biggest setting up you have had recently."

He marched me over, and as we entered, Old Dan looked up and, addressing my escort, asked, "What are you here for? What do you want?" "I found this man running at large without a pass, and thought it was my duty to bring him here." "Without a pass? Was he making any disturbance?" "No sir." "And so you arrest one of your own regiment because he happens to be without a pass and then come here to interrupt me. If you come here again on such an errand I will put you in the guard house. Go to your post."

After my escort had gone out with a flea in his ear, Capt. Dan removed his spectacles, and wiping his eyes, which a good deal resembled gashes cut in ripe tomatoes, pointed to the table, saying, "I reckon there is something left in the bottle, help yourself." I did as the captain requested. After chatting a little with him, a couple of officers came in, and I touched my cap, bade the captain good-day and made my escape.

POOR WHITE TRASH.

Among the white people about here, are very few who would be ranked among the first or even second class. Nearly all of them are what is called the poor white trash or clay-eaters. I am told they actually do eat clay, a habit they contract like any other bad habit. Now I cannot vouch for the truth of this, never having seen them eating it, but some of them look as though that was about all they had to eat. They are an utterly ignorant set, scarcely able to make themselves intelligible, and in many ways they are below the negroes in intelligence and manner of living, but perhaps they are not wholly to blame for it, the same principle that will oppress a black man, will a white one. They are entirely cut off from the means of acquiring land or an education, even though they wished to. Public schools are unknown here and land can only be purchased by the plantation. That leaves them in rather a bad fix; poor, shiftless and ignorant. Their highest ambition is to hunt, fish, drink whiskey and toady to their masters. You speak to one of them and he will look at you in a listless sort of way as though unable or undecided whether to answer or not. Ask one of them the distance across the river, and he will either say he don't know, or "it is right smart." Ask one of them the distance to any place or house out in the country, and he will tell you it is "a right smart step," or "you go up yer a right smart step, and you will come to a creek," and from there it will be so many looks and a screech; meaning from the creek that number of angles in the road and as far beyond as the voice will reach. They do not seem to have any intelligent idea about anything, and in talking with the cusses, one scarcely knows whether to pity them or be amused.

SNUFF DIPPING.

The women here have a filthy habit of snuff chewing or dipping as they call it, and I am told it is practiced more or less by all classes of women. The manner of doing it is simple enough: they take a small stick or twig about two inches long, of a certain kind of bush, and chew one end of it until it becomes like a brush. This they dip into the snuff and then put it in their mouths. After chewing a while they remove the stick and expectorate about a gill, and repeat the operation. Many of the women among the clay-eaters chew plug tobacco and can squirt the juice through their teeth as far and as straight as the most accomplished chewer among the lords of creation.

MY DIARY.

GROWING TIRED.

APRIL 25. We have now been several weeks in the city and the boys are beginning to tire of it. This every-day, humdrum life is getting irksome, and the boys are anxious for a change. Frequent changes and excitement are what keeps up the soldier's spirits. In the dull routine and idleness of camp, they grow uneasy, homesick and despondent.

FORT MACON.

MAY 1. Martial law not being a very favorable institution for pleasure parties, I presume the usual May day festival is dispensed with here as I have not seen any parties out or demonstrations of any kind going on. I should think a May party here might be very successful as the woods abound with wild flowers in great variety and beauty.

Fort Macon surrendered to Gen. Burnside last Friday evening, after a bombardment of eleven hours. The general succeeded in getting his siege guns in battery behind some sand ridges about half a mile in rear of the fort, unobserved by the garrison, and the first notice they had of his presence was a shot from one of the guns. After holding out for eleven hours and seeing they could make no defense and that there was no chance for escape, they hauled down their colors. By this surrender, 65 guns and 450 prisoners, with stores and ammunition, have fallen into our hands. Their loss was eight killed and twenty wounded. Our loss was one killed and five wounded.

A good story is told in connection with the surrender of this fort to the Confederates. After the war broke out and they were seizing the forts, a strong force of Confederates, with a great flourish of trumpets, presented themselves one morning at the sallyport of the fort, demanding its immediate and unconditional surrender. Now it happened that the only occupants of the fort were an old ordnance sergeant and his wife who had been in charge of the property for many years. The old sergeant came to the gate, and looking over the crowd, said to the officer in command that under the circumstances he thought the garrison might as well surrender, but he would like the privilege of taking the old flag and marching out with the honors of war. To this the officer assented and the old sergeant hauled down the flag and winding it around him, he and his wife marched out, greatly to the surprise of the officer, who found that they two comprised the whole garrison.

MAY 8. Our city life is about over; we have orders to break up housekeeping here tomorrow and go on a rusticating tour in the country. Among the boys all is speculation as to where we are going and what our errand is.

A TRIP INTO THE COUNTRY.

MAY 9. After nearly two months of scrubbing and cleaning, with new caps and pants, the 25th regiment stands in column of platoons on Pollock street, as tony a looking regiment as there is in the service. The colonel and staff with the band take the head of the column, and amid the cheers of hundreds of darkies, the march commences. Leaving the city we soon enter the woods, and after marching about three miles, come out to a cotton plantation. Here we make a short halt and look over the place. It looks rather run down, the house is old and out of repair, the negro quarters are built of logs, and look as though they were hardly habitable. But I presume everything on a plantation has to correspond. The gentlemanly proprietor, whoever he was, has left, taking with him the best of his servants, leaving here a few old ones to shift for themselves.

A few miles further on, we came to another cotton plantation. This presented a better appearance, a neat cottage house, painted white with green blinds, good barns and surroundings. The negro quarters were comfortable looking houses, built of boards, with glass windows, and whitewashed. This gentleman with his servants had also gone up the country. About two miles further on, at a fork of the road, we found the 17th Massachusetts, Col. Amory, doing picket duty. Here a road branched to the right leading into the woods, which we took, following it about four miles, coming out at a small clearing, where was a little red house and log barn, with a few negro cabins. This is known as the Red house, and we relieve the 23d Massachusetts, which is doing picket duty. And this then is to be our home for a while. It certainly is retired and rural, not another house within four miles of us. The clearing is not over twelve or fifteen acres in extent, with a small creek running through it. Woods to the right of us, woods to the left of us, woods to the front of us, woods all around us. This surely must be the place for which Cowper sighed, when he wrote,

"O! for a lodge in some vast wilderness."

After getting a little rested from the long march, we pitched our tents in a field a short distance from the house. The colonel and his family, with the band, pitched their camp in the large shady yard next to the house. The tents up, the picket guard is detailed and posted; a part of them along the road we came up, and connecting with the 17th Massachusetts, a part along the road to the right, and connecting with the 27th Massachusetts stationed at Batchellor's creek, and the balance along the roads and horse paths leading into Dixie. The tents up, the pickets out, dress parade and supper over, I reckon the country must be safe for one night at least, and I will improve it by trying to get some sleep and rest, for it will be just my luck to be on the detail tomorrow.

MR. BOGEY.

MAY 11. This place is what is called a turpentine plantation, where they get the pitch from which turpentine is distilled. The owner, Mr. Bogey, a harmless, inoffensive old gentleman, claims to be a Union man, and I reckon he is, because he does not run away or seem to be afraid of us. He tells me he owns 2000 acres of land, nearly all turpentine forest, and has 10,000 trees running pitch. He said the war had ruined him and thinks it has the whole south. He said the rebels had taken all but one of his horses and about everything else he had that they wanted. His niggers had all left him and gone down town. He expected that when we came, but cared very little about it, as he had only a few and they were about as much trouble and expense to him as they were worth. He said he was getting old, his business was all broke up and by the time the war was over and things settled he would be too old for anything. I asked him if all those pigs running about in the woods were his. He reckoned they were. I inquired if he knew how many he had. He couldn't tell exactly, but reckoned there was right smart. The thought occurred to me that if that was as near as he could tell, if a few of them were gobbled they would never be missed, provided the squeal could be shut off quick enough. I learn that Gen. Burnside has given Mr. Bogey a protection, whatever that is. That perhaps may do well enough for him, but I should not want to warrant it a sure thing for all these pigs and sheep running about here.

CAMP BULLOCK.

Our camp is named Camp Bullock, in honor of Alex. H. Bullock of Worcester, Mass. Today the boys are busy writing letters home, and it troubles them to tell where to date their letters from. They invent all sorts of names; some of them with a romantic turn of mind, date from Camp Rural, Woodlawn, Forestdale, Riverdale, etc., but Mason, with a more practical turn of mind, dates his from Hell Centre. The boys who were out in the woods last night say it is great fun, although they were not disturbed; there is just enough excitement and mosquitoes to keep them from getting drowsy.

PICKET DUTY.

MAY 14. I was out in the woods yesterday and last night on picket duty, and picket duty is simply lying around in the brush watching the approach of outside parties. Parties approaching in the night time and failing to promptly respond to the hail of the picket are given an instantaneous passport to a land that is fairer than this. A picket is composed of three or more men stationed at convenient distances from each other along the roads, horse paths and anywhere an enemy might be supposed to come. One keeps watch while the others sleep, but with the hooting of the owls, sand-fleas, woodticks, lizards and mosquitoes, their repose is a good deal disturbed.

A SCOUTING PARTY.

Yesterday Col. Upton with a strong scouting party went out

to Tuscarora, a little hamlet about five miles distant, where is the enemy's outpost and where is kept a party of observation. On the approach of the colonel and his party they left, but before doing so set fire to a new steam saw and grain mill which was destroyed. Mr. Bogey was a good deal vexed at the destruction of this mill. He said it was built only two years ago at a cost of $5000 and was a great accommodation to the people here abouts, and he, with other farmers, put in their money to help build it. These people have a great notion of burning their property on our approach. I really cannot understand it. They ought to know that it is of no use to us, and in the end will be a sore loss to them.

WE GO OUT MAKING CALLS.

MAY 16. For some time past the pickets of the 17th Massachusetts have been a good deal troubled by being fired on in the night. The enemy's cavalry would come down, a few of them dismount and creeping up would fire on them. They would sometimes have cow bells with them, in order to divert attention and get nearer. But the boys soon learned that dodge, and when they heard a cow bell, would draw their straightest bead on it and let fly. In this state of affairs it was thought best to make those fellows a call, and if they wanted anything of us to give them an opportunity to take it. So, yesterday morning, we marched out to the Trent road, where we joined the 17th Massachusetts, with five companies of the 3d New York cavalry and a section of a battery, the whole under command of Col. Amory, of the 17th. The cavalry taking the advance, we marched up the road a couple of miles, coming to a deep gully or ravine; crossing this, the advance cavalry guard soon came upon the enemy's pickets, driving them in and beyond their station into a swamp, where they formed an ambuscade, thinking there was only a small cavalry force and that they might capture them. By this time the infantry had come up to their rendezvous, which was a large, nice house, with ample barn room for their horses. Thinking this was too good accommodation for them and too near our line, it was set on fire and burned. We now heard firing ahead and hurried on. They had closed around the advance cavalry guard, and commenced the fight. The other companies being close by soon took a hand in it and were giving them about all they wanted when the infantry came up. When they saw the infantry and artillery they took to their heels towards Trenton, a small village a few miles distant.

Col. Upton wanted to follow them up and give them some more, but Col. Amory being in command, thought we had accomplished our purpose and had better return. In this skirmish the enemy lost eight killed and two prisoners, one of them wounded. Our cavalry had two wounded. The wounded men were brought out and loaded into an ambulance. When they brought out the wounded rebel they put down the stretcher on which he was lying near where I was standing. He was a smooth-faced, fair-haired boy, and was moaning piteously with pain from a bullet wound in his head, and asking himself what his mother would say when she heard of it. His thoughts turned on his home and of his mother. I pitied the boy, but could not help thinking, as a cavalryman told him, he should have thought of that before being caught here. We arrived back in camp late in the afternoon, tired, hungry and covered with mud. I reckon they will not disturb our pickets any more at present in the way they have done. Creeping up in the dark and firing on a lone picket is mean and cowardly. If they want anything of us let them come in force and get it; that is proper and honorable.

REASONING.

MAY 20. Lying around here in the woods, hearing no sound but the moaning of the wind through the tree tops, is rather dull business. There is nothing in it that inspires any lofty, rapturous thought, and yet it inspires thought, and already one of Mr. Bogey's sheep has fallen a victim to thoughts inspired by the soughing of the wind through this dark forest shutting out the day; I reckon it will not be necessary to say anything to Mr. Bogey about it, as he is a loyal man, and, as the lawyers say, the presumption is he would be more than glad to contribute a mutton in suppression of this unholy rebellion.

THE PINE FORESTS.

The woods here abound in timber of the finest description, many of the trees attaining a height of more than 100 feet. It is seldom one is seen of more than two feet in diameter at its base, tapering but slightly and without limbs for a distance of from 60 to 80 feet. I have seen some that would square fifteen inches, 80 feet from the stump. These are the turpentine trees, and the pitch, or turpentine as it is called, is obtained by cutting a wide, deep box at the base of the tree capable of holding two or three quarts of the pitch. From each corner of the box the bark is stripped off, coming to a point about three feet above the box. This is done when the tree is first boxed. The next year about three feet more of the bark is removed, coming to a point as before. This process goes on until the tree is blazed for a distance of 20 or more feet, and can be done on the east, south and west sides of the trees. The tree will run pitch quite a number of years before it dies, and is then called lightwood, and is either split up into rails or converted into tar. The pitch that runs into the boxes is dipped out into barrels, and is called dip or virgin turpentine, while that which adheres to the tree is scraped off and is called scrape, and is less valuable than the dip. The pitch is barreled up and sold to the distillers. Tar is obtained by cutting the lightwood into lengths of about eight feet and split fine; a tunnel-shaped hole is dug in the ground, with the center about three feet deep, and from the center a drain runs to a barrel or vat sunk low enough in the ground to receive the tar as it runs from the kiln. The wood is packed in this hole with the ends to the center, keeping the center lowest; when all the wood required for the kiln is piled up, the sides and top are plastered over with clay, and the fire kindled on top. The fire smouldering down through the pile, tries out the tar, which settling to the bottom, runs out into the vat, and is then barreled. A kiln will run from ten to twenty barrels according to size.

THUNDER STORMS.

MAY 28. It has rained almost constantly for the past week, and when it rains here in Dixie it is no drizzle, but comes down a perfect waterfall, sometimes for twelve hours together, accompanied with lightning and thunder of the grandest description. There is a grandeur in one of these storms at night, when in the woods among the tall pines, far away from the camp on picket, that no person can form much of an idea of unless they have been there to witness it. On such a night the solitude is awfully impressive, the picket stands concealed behind a tree in the drenching rain, solitary and alone, absorbed only in his own reflections and looking out for the lurking foe. The vivid lightning with almost continuous flashes illumines the grand old woods, while peal after peal of deafening thunder breaks, rolls and rumbles athwart the sky, sending back its echoes, as though an hundred batteries filled the air. Although there is a grandeur beyond description on such a night, there are very few of the boys, however, who care enough about witnessing it to be very anxious about going. But it has got to be done, and somebody has got it to do, so after the detail is made, they go off cheerfully, consoling themselves with the thought that they can have all the whiskey they want when they get back the next morning.

CHAPTER IV.

A CHANGE OF BASE.

JUNE 1. And now something else has turned up, and here we are encamped just outside the city and behind our batteries. The order to move took us by surprise, as the first notice we had was to pick up our traps and be ready to march in half an hour. At the time appointed everything was packed and loaded on the wagons and we were on the march. Dark found us here with our tents up ready for housekeeping, and our coffee boiling for supper. All this and a march of twelve miles in one afternoon. Two companies, G and K, are left back for a few days, and are assisted by cavalry. All the advance regiments are drawn in behind the forts and the whole division, with the exception of three regiments, are now here. I have heard no reason why the division is concentrated, but perhaps the general expects company and intends to be in readiness to give them a right royal reception. Our line of defenses extends from the Neuse to the Trent rivers, a distance of about one mile, and on the line are three forts mounting in all 32 guns. There are also eleven light batteries of six guns each, with gunboats on the rivers that have an enfilading range in front of the line. With 10,000 troops behind the works, with a wide open field in front, it looks as though our position was a pretty safe one, and if anybody comes here with any hostile intent, hell will begin to fill up pretty soon after they get within the range of our guns. Our life up in the woods, on the whole was rather a pleasant one; I reckon the boys rather enjoyed it and were in no hurry about leaving. There was less restraint on them, they could do a little more as they pleased and were free from the drills, parades, red tape and formalities of the regular camp, with just enough excitement about it to keep them from getting dreary and homesick.

CAMP OLIVER.

JUNE 6. We are now in a neatly arranged camp on somewhat elevated ground at the west side of the city, and about a quarter of a mile to the rear of Fort Totten, a large field fortification mounting twenty heavy guns. A back street runs along the left flank, on which is situated the guard quarters, and a line of sentinels extends along it. This camp is named Camp Oliver, in honor of Gen. Oliver of Salem, Mass., formerly adjutant-general of that state. We can now brush ourselves up and settle down to the dull routine of camp life—Drills, parades, reviews, inspections, guard duty, fatigue duty and all manner of things which come under the head of a well ordered camp. Our two companies left at Red house are drawn in about five miles, and are now at the Jackson place on the Trent road. That brings them within easy distance. They can be easily reinforced in case of attack or make their own way back to camp. The Red house is again in the enemy's country, but Mr. Bogey is not there; he thought he had rather live under the old flag and take his chances, and so moved with us into town.

HOT WEATHER.

JUNE 16. It is so hot most of the time we are scarcely able to do anything more than keep ourselves as comfortable as possible. All duty is suspended except guard duty and dress parade, and we are getting almost too lazy to eat; in fact do miss a good many meals unless they happen to have something we like. We lie around in our tents or in the shade of the trees from 9 o'clock in the morning till 4 in the afternoon, brushing away the flies, and trying to keep cool. I thought I had seen some flies at home but they are no comparison to what we have here. I really believe there are more flies in this camp than there are in the whole state of Massachusetts. Besides they are regular secesh ones, and by the way they bite, one would think he was among a nest of hornets. I am often reminded of the old minstrel song:

"If you perchance in summer time
Should visit Carolina's sultry clime,
And in the shade should chance to lie
You'd soon find out the blue tail fly."

We were visited last evening by a thunder storm which makes it quite comfortable today. For several days past the weather has been very hot, the thermometer ranging about 100 degrees in the shade. Just before sunset last evening the clouds began to gather and we soon heard the low mutterings of thunder. We knew very well what that meant and set about fastening our tents by driving down the pins a little firmer. We got ready for it just in season, and such a storm! a regular bombardment, with rivers of water, lasting about two hours. Why our thunder storms at home are only a slight skirmish compared with this. After four or five days so hot we can but just live we get one of these storms, and then we have one cool, comfortable day. It is so cool today I expect the colonel will have us out for drill towards night. He says when it is cool we must work a little or we shall get so lazy we can't stir, and will forget all we ever knew.

DRESS PARADE.

Next to a good choir of singers, the colonel takes great pride in a dress parade; and he certainly has good ones, as good, perhaps, as any regiment here. The boys like to please him and at dress parade put in their best work, especially if there happens to be a good many looking on. They have got so used to him, they can anticipate the order, and it is executed together as one man. I reckon Gen. Foster thinks pretty well of us, as he is out here two or three times a week to witness our dress parades.

AN EXCURSION.

June 29. Companies C and B, together with Capt. Schenck's New York battery company as infantry, returned yesterday afternoon from an expedition across the Neuse river, having been gone three days. We crossed the river Thursday morning, the 26th, and started out on a reconnoissance, tour of observation, scout, raid or whatever else it might be called, Capt. Schenck in command. We penetrated into the country some four or five miles, coming out at a cross road. There in the shade of the woods we halted for rest and lunch. Put out a few pickets to prevent surprise. I should think they were out about twelve rods from the column, which made it comparatively safe. After a little time, and while we were having a kind of picnic, there was a stir among the pickets in the rear and it was reported they had made a capture. The authorities went out to see what was up, and soon returned with an old horse and cart containing a few bags of meal and driven by a couple of grown-up girls, or more properly speaking, young ladies. They were returning from mill and were pretty badly frightened on finding themselves prisoners of war. The officers behaved towards them with the utmost gallantry, assuring them that no harm should come to them. On these assurances they were soon comforted and seemed to regard it as rather a good joke. After holding them close prisoners of war about a couple of hours, they were paroled and allowed to go their way.

We resumed our march and about two miles farther on came out at another cross road. Here we left a few pickets and proceeding a mile or so farther, came out to Latham's plantation. This is the finest plantation I have yet seen, a large two-story modern-built house, with large, nice lawns and surroundings, the road and driveways set with shade and ornamental trees, and everything kept up sleek and nice, showing thrift, wealth and refinement. Here on the lawn in front of the house, we bivouacked for the night. This Latham is a battery captain in the Confederate service, and we had a hack at him, capturing his battery at the battle before Newbern. He is now somewhere in the Confederacy, but just where deponent saith not. Mrs. Latham was greatly surprised at seeing us, and had made no preparations to receive us. To relieve her embarrassment as much as possible, the boys left her to entertain the officers in the mansion while we took care of ourselves. The boys brought from the barn about two tons of husks and corn leaves, spreading them under the rose-trees on the lawn for beds. They then milked the cows, killed the chickens and pigs, emptied the hives of their honey and made all necessary preparations for our comfort during our stay. The darky women in the kitchen were kept busy with their fry-pans, hoe-cakes and coffee-pots until a late hour in the night, and never before were there guests at Latham's whom they were more pleased to see or more willing to serve. This was truly the land flowing with milk and honey, and the boys revelled in luxury far into the night, after which they sought rest and repose under the roses. In the morning, the darky women asked if they might go with us over to Newbern. They were told they might and to pick up their traps and follow along. As we were about leaving, Mrs. Latham inquired of Capt. Schenck who was to pay her for the damage we had done. The captain told her to make out her bill and one of these days Uncle Sam and Latham would have a settlement, and she could then work it in. As we moved out of the yard we were joined by the darky women, toting big bundles on their heads. Mrs. Latham came running down the lawn, shouting after them at the top of her voice, "Here, Kitty, Peggy, Rosa, Dinah, where are you going with those horrid men? Come right back here this minute!" The women, looking back over their shoulders and showing immense rows of ivory, replied to her, "Goo-bye, missus, goo-bye! spec we'es gwine ober to Newbern; goo-bye, missus, goo-bye!" and we marched off down the road, leaving Mrs. Latham alone to reflect on the vicissitudes incident to a state of war. I must needs say, however, that after being so hospitably entertained, it was a rascally, mean trick to run off the servants and leave our sleeping apartments in such a disordered condition. But then, Latham had no business to be away from home. He should have been there, ready to entertain company.

Arriving back at the cross roads, we found the boys all right and gave them a share of the good things they had been deprived of the night before. We stayed here all day and night, and not seeing or hearing anything, returned to camp yesterday afternoon. What the results of this expedition will be, remains for the future historian to record. The trophies were two prisoners of war paroled, four darky women, one horse, a big yellow dog and lots of fun. What the object of this expedition was, I presume will always remain among the mysteries of this cruel war, but there is little doubt but the object was accomplished, as the generals say.

CELEBRATING THE FOURTH OF JULY.

JULY 5. The Fourth was celebrated with salutes from the forts, batteries and gunboats, morning, noon and night. There were gala times in Camp Oliver last night. A huge bonfire was set from a pyramid of 75 barrels of resin, and when well on fire it lighted up the camp in grand style. All the regimental bands were present, and under the direction of P. S. Gilmore, leader of the 24th Massachusetts regimental band, were consolidated, and gave a grand concert with artillery accompaniment. The effect was very fine. The camp guard was taken off and all went in for a good time. The parade ground was covered with officers and soldiers from other camps, and officers and marines from the boats and citizens generally. The delighted darkies were on hand in force. It far surpassed anything they had ever heard or dreamed of. They are very fond of music, and gathered in great numbers in the vicinity of the bands, never noticing the battery which stood a short distance away, or if they did it was a sealed book to them and a harmless looking battery enough. After the bands had played a few selections they struck up Hail Columbia; and when in quick succession three or four of those guns were let off, there was a great scarcity of darkies. They are terribly frightened at artillery firing, and will make the distance between themselves and the guns as far and as quick as possible. The celebration was kept up till near midnight; everybody seemed to enjoy it and had a good time. If we were behind Boston in orations, floral exhibitions and the like of that, we certainly were ahead of them in music, salutes and fireworks.

COMPANY DRILLS.

JULY 25. The colonel, thinking that guard duty and dress

parades are not quite exercise enough for us, has ordered company drills in the forenoon. The company officers do not take very kindly to this, and thinking it a good opportunity to give the sergeants a little practice in drilling the companies, they shirk out of it every time they can invent an excuse to do so. The companies are seen out under command of the orderlies or some other of the sergeants frequently. B company moves out of the company street on to the parade ground, and after executing a few brilliant maneuvers, starts off across the fields to the Trent road, a little out of sight of the camp, and here in the shade of the trees we sit down and await the recall, when we march back into camp with all the pomp and circumstance of glorious war. The duty has been performed and everybody seems well enough satisfied, except perhaps the performers.

PATRIOTISM SUPPRESSED.

And now, right here under the broad banner of freedom, personal liberty and rising patriotism has been suppressed. A party of small darky boys organized themselves into a drum corps and furnished themselves with old tin pans and kettles for an outfit. Being natural musicians, they soon acquired the art of drumming, and when they thought they could make a creditable appearance before the public appeared one evening, standing just outside the guard in front of our dress parade. When the band led off down the line the little fellows commenced putting in their work, and they certainly did a good job, as they beat the time very well. But the thing was so ludicrous it was with difficulty the band could perform their part, and many of the boys in the line could not restrain their laughter. The little fellows seemed to enjoy it immensely, and would put in an appearance every evening, until the colonel finding it impossible to have a decent dress parade ordered the guard officers to suppress the amateur band, very much I presume against his inclination and feelings.

MISS FOSTER.

Gen. Foster has his wife and daughter with him here, which must make it very agreeable for him. Mrs. Foster is engaged in works of love and mercy around the hospitals, while Miss Foster, a young lady of some 16 or 17 years, is pretty much engaged in horseback riding and having a good time generally. She is quite a military character, as we notice that when she and the general ride past here, she always returns the salutes from the sentinels as gracefully as the general. She frequently rides past here alone, and the sentinels along the street take great pride in honoring her with a present arms, a compliment which she never fails to acknowledge by a graceful wave of her hand and her face wreathed with smiles.

I GET ON THE RETIRED LIST.

AUGUST 29. Until recently I have been quite a popular commander of Sunday church parties. The boys would get up their parties and get me a pass to take them into town to church. I would take them in and, halting on some convenient corner, would deliver myself of a little speech. I would say, "Boys, I have always believed in the largest tolerance in matters of religion and politics, and as much as I should like to have you attend church with me, if you have any preferences you are at liberty to enjoy them; far be it from me to impose my authority on your feelings or conscience. I shall expect you on the corner at the appointed time that we may report back in camp in season for dress parade." Now, if they couldn't have had a tolerably good time under those conditions, it certainly was no fault of mine. But this, like every other good thing, could not always last. One Sunday afternoon, when we gathered on the corner, one of the party failed to put in an appearance. After waiting beyond a reasonable time, he was defaulted and we returned to camp. About night he came in, showing unmistakable signs of having been on the hardest kind of fatigue duty. Instead of going to his quarters as he was told to, he thought it was his duty to interview the captain. That interview resulted in a court martial, before which I was ordered to appear. I was asked numerous questions, all of which I answered to the best of my knowledge and belief, and my evidence not only convicted the prisoner but reflected somewhat on myself, for in summing it up, they somehow fixed it up in such a way as to make it appear that I was in the practice of taking parties into town on Sundays, ostensibly to church and then letting them go wherever they pleased, and inquired of me if that was not about the true solution of the problem. Wishing to avoid controversy, I assented. I was then told that I could retire from that august presence, a privilege of which I availed myself immediately, but what I noticed as being rather singular, after that little interview I was in command of no more Sunday parties.

WE LOSE OUR BANDS.

SEPT. 20. All the regimental bands have been mustered out and have gone home. Ours left the first of this month, and it seems quite lonely to have them gone. They were the solace of many a weary hour. I understand that this is in the interest of economy, the bands costing so much it was thought best to let them go. I also learn that the officers' pay has been raised, so just where the saving comes in does not appear. As I am only an enlisted man I am not supposed to see things quite so clearly, so I presume it is all right any way, but we think it is rather sharp economy.

A TRIP TO PLYMOUTH, N. C.

On the 15th of this month, the 25th, Major Pickett in command, with the 17th Massachusetts and the 10th Connecticut regiments, the whole under command of Col. Upton, embarked on steamers bound for Plymouth, on the Roanoke river which empties into the Albemarle sound at its extreme western end. On the morning of the 16th we passed Roanoke island, and our attention was attracted towards it as being the scene of our first conflict and success. We soon afterward entered the Albemarle sound, a beautiful sheet of water running east and west, about 70 miles long with an average width of some 20 miles. It was a beautiful day, and the sail, as we slowly steamed along, was delightful, affording us a fine view of the shores. The shores were in striking contrast; the south shore is low and swampy, rising scarcely out of the water, while the north is bold, with a gently rising slope and shows many handsome farms. The scenery here is the first that has reminded us of home, and looks as though it was inhabited by a better class of people than we have yet seen.

About dusk we reach the upper end of the sound, and turning sharply to the left, enter the woods, where the overhanging branches of the tall trees seem almost to embrace each other. We are now in the Roanoke river, which is here quite narrow. In the dusk of the evening, as we grope our way along the narrow channel through the trees, the scenery is grandly wild. Some five or six miles through the woods brought us to the little town of Plymouth, situated on the left or south bank of the river. Here we drop anchor for the night, and wait until morning to learn more of our excursion.

The next morning we learned the expedition had been given up, and we steamed back down the river on our return trip, without scarcely getting a glimpse of Plymouth. On coming out into the sound we could see the little town of Edenton on the north shore, hid away in a little nook of the sound, and almost buried in trees. From our standpoint it looked like a charming little town. It is occasionally occupied by our troops and the gunboats make frequent calls there. The only setback to the pleasure of the trip down the sound was the annoyance caused the officers by the hilarity of the boys who entered into the spirit of fun and seemed to be bent on having a general good time. The officers occupied the saloon and were greatly disturbed by the noise and racket on deck over their heads. They would often send up and order the boys to keep more quiet as the noise disturbed them. The boys of course would respect their wishes, and for a time all would be quiet, but soon another party would come on deck, from some other part of the boat, and bedlam would again break loose. The officers had my commiseration; I exercised all my authority to preserve order and would willingly have done anything that lay in my power to have alleviated their sufferings, for it is not surprising that men brought up in machine shops, rolling mills, foundries and like places should be possessed of rather sensitive nerves.

We arrived back at Newbern, the morning of the 18th, having had a pleasant excursion of about 400 miles, and if we could have had our band with us the thing would have been complete. It seems the object of our visit to Plymouth was for the officers of the expedition to consult with the military and naval officers at that station in regard to the expediency of dislodging the enemy's forces at Rainbow bluff, a point some 30 miles up the river, which prevents our boats from ascending higher up, and which they cannot shell out. At the council of officers it was decided that if we should succeed in capturing it, it would be without results, as it is of no military consequence to us, and that it would be unwise to risk men in an enterprise that would be barren in results. Hence our return to Newbern.

COL. UPTON LEAVES US.

OCT. 29. Our regiment is now left with only one field officer, Major Pickett. Col. Upton left us yesterday and Lieut. Col. Sprague and Adjutant Harkness left us two weeks ago. Lieut. Col. Sprague left to take command of a nine months' regiment already recruited in the city of Worcester. Adjutant Harkness is commissioned major of the same regiment. Col. Upton resigned on account of failing health, which I hope he may speedily recover after reaching home. All three of these officers have had the confidence and respect of the regiment in a marked degree, and our best wishes attend them in other fields. As a slight token of their regard for Col. Upton, the enlisted men are having manufactured a $1000 sword, which they intend to present to him. Major Pickett will succeed to the coloneley, and according to military usage, Capt. Moulton of company H will be lieutenant colonel and Capt. Atwood of company C will be major. This will fill the field again, and occasion some changes and promotions in the line. I reckon if I was of an ambitious turn of mind, I should aspire to some of these places of honor and emolument, but remembering the promise that whoever humbleth himself shall be exalted, I will continue to wait on.

REINFORCEMENTS.

Massachusetts boys are getting thick as blueberries about here, and we are glad to see them. Three regiments of nine months' troops have just arrived, the 3d, 5th and 44th regiments, and I hear that more are coming. A good many of the new comers have called on us and seem desirous of making our acquaintance, to which we are not averse, seeing they are good appearing fellows and have plenty of money, which is not a bad qualification, especially when introduced to the sutler. I learn that Gen. Foster leaves tomorrow on an expedition, taking with him nearly all the force here, including the three new regiments. That will be breaking them in pretty quick after getting here. They, of course, have not had much drill and probably half of them never fired a gun. But to us, a little trip up the country is cheering news. After being shut up in camp so long any change is gladly accepted.

THE TARBORO MARCH.

Nov. 12. On the morning of Oct. 30, Major Pickett, with six companies (the other four being on picket up the Trent road), left Newbern, embarking on the steamer Highlander for Washington on the Pamlico river. Here we joined Gen. Foster's expedition for a raid up the country. The force consisted of the 17th, 23d, 24th and 25th Massachusetts and 10th Connecticut regiments of three years' troops, and the 3d, 5th and 44th Massachusetts regiments of nine months' troops, with five batteries of the 3d New York artillery, Capt. Belgers' Rhode Island battery and seven companies of the 3d New York cavalry, besides a heavy wagon and ambulance train.

On Sunday morning Nov. 2, the expedition left Washington for a march across the country to the Roanoke river. The 23d and 25th were detailed as guard over the wagon and ambulance train. We marched through a poor and sparsely populated section of country without interruption or anything to create excitement, until about the middle of the afternoon, when we heard firing on the advance. They had reached a swamp of considerable width, with a small creek running across and overflowing the road for quite a distance. At this point two regiments of the enemy disputed the passage of the swamp, and a brisk infantry and artillery fire commenced, which lasted with short intervals for an hour or more, when the cavalry and two batteries charged across. The enemy beat a precipitate retreat, greatly accelarated by shells from the batteries. Our loss was small, not over a dozen killed and wounded, and most of these were from the 44th Massachusetts, which behaved nobly.

During this skirmish the wagon train made slow progress, advancing a short distance and then halting. It was late in the evening when we reached the swamp. All the troops were on the other side, but we got orders to halt where we were over night. The mules were fed and we made a supper of cold meat, hardtack and coffee, after which we lay down by the side of the fence to sleep.

MULES IN A MUDHOLE.

Next morning the mule teams commenced the passage of the swamp and mudhole. Hearing a great noise and shouting, I went down to see what was up. I mounted the rude foot bridge at the side, improvised for the benefit of pedestrians, and walked along until I was near the middle of the mudhole and where the creek crossed the road. Here was a file of men on each side of the road, armed with hoop-poles and standing in mud and water from six inches to three feet deep. When a team was driven in, it received all necessary encouragement from the hoop-poles and strong lungs of the men while running the gauntlet. If the pilot was skilful and kept on the corduroy, the passage would be made before the mules would get discouraged. Sometimes the mules would get off the corduroy, but if the wagon kept on, the mules would manage to flounder back and go on. After a spell a careless driver ran his wagon off the corduroy and down it went to the axle. Here was a pretty fix. The mules couldn't haul it out and no other team could get by. It was decided to unload the wagon, so the mules could pull it out. The load, consisting of beef and hardtack, was dumped into the creek, but the mules knew nothing of this arrangement, they only knew they were hopelessly stuck, and when they were appealed to to haul out the wagon, they obstinately refused; bracing out their forelegs and sticking their ears straight up in the air, they seemed to proclaim themselves a fixture. No amount of swearing and belaboring them with hoop-poles had the slightest effect. Capt. Schenck, who was standing by watching the fun, told them he would hitch on one of his teams and haul them out. The captain had a battery of 20-pounder Napoleon guns, with teams of eight heavy horses. He ordered in one of the teams and told them to hitch on to the mules, and when all was ready, he would give the order. When all was ready, the captain yelled, "Forward, march!". The horses, understanding the order, stepped smartly off; while the mules, not understanding it, did not keep step with the horses, but standing there braced out, the heels of three or four of them went up in the air, and they came down on their heads; in this way, sometimes under water and sometimes out, kicking and floundering, trying to regain their feet, they were dragged out through the mudhole, to the great delight and amusement of the captain and all other spectators.

This place is known as Rawls' Mills creek, and that a grateful posterity may better understand the situation, I quote from Longfellow or some other fellow:

> Then the muels strove and tugged,
> Up the hillsides steep and rugged,
> Till they came unto a mudhole;
> This was nary a common puddle,
> One it was without a bottom,
> Into which the muels, rot 'em,
> Got so very far deluded,
> Nothing but their ears protruded,
> Picturing in a situation
> Uncle Abe's administration.

DARKIES AND MULES.

All the teams across, the march was resumed through a much better country, and we reached Williamston on the Roanoke river, about noon. Our teams are four horse and six mule teams. Some of the mule teams are driven by darkies, who sit on the nigh hind mule and pilot the craft by means of a single line running to the leaders, called a jerk line. With this line and their peculiar mule dialect, they handle the team admirably. Darkies and mules work together naturally; they understand each other perfectly and have the same dialect. Take a mule team that a white man can do nothing with, and let a darky come along and speak to them; in a minute they are entirely different animals and as docile as a kitten. They seem to have a love for him and are perfectly cognizant of all his actions and movements. If a darky while driving falls asleep, the mules know it in a minute and will stop. The leaders will face about and commence tangling themselves up in the chains and gearing of the next pair, and that will go on until some one hits the nigger on his head with a pine knot or lump of clay, waking him up. He will give the line a few jerks and call out to the mules in their language, and they will untangle themselves, straighten out and go on as though nothing had happened. Niggers and mules are a great institution.

Williamston is a pretty little town of about 1200 or 1500 inhabitants, nearly all of whom had left, leaving it to the tender mercies of an army; of course what was left lying around loose was gobbled up. When the wagon train marched through, the boys were frying the chickens and pigs in the streets, and probably the houses and stores contributed to their wants. The train halted just outside the town till about 4 p. m., when we again resumed the march, going up the Hamilton road. We went up this road about ten miles, and bivouacked in a large field of corn about 10 p. m. This afforded abundant forage for our horses and mules, also good beds and fires for ourselves. This day's march was through a fine section of country and without opposition. A great quantity of corn was yet unharvested and a few barnsful of harvested corn which we found was set on fire, as being the best and quickest way to market it.

PLANTATION DANCE.

Soon after we got into camp, a few darkies were seen lurking around, not knowing exactly whether it would do to come too near. But their fears were soon dispelled by a few darkies who were with us, telling them "de Yankees are our frien's," and to come right along. They soon began to flock into camp, and in a little while a hundred or more had come in. After the boys had their suppers, large fires were kindled, around which 200 or 300 of the boys formed a ring and getting thirty or forty of these darkies, men and women, inside, set them to dancing. They were free then and seemed anxious to do anything to please the boys and keep on good terms with them. Three or four of them would pat the time and the rest would dance. They seemed to enjoy the fun as much as the spectators. Here was a genuine plantation dance in costume; men and women were dressed in well-worn garments of gunny cloth or Kentucky jeans, with enormous brogan shoes of russet leather, some of them looking as though they had a whole tannery on their feet. Some of the old ones were a little lame and would try to get rid of dancing by saying they didn't know how, but the boys would tell them they did and that they must go in. It was great sport to watch the antics they cut up trying to dance. The next morning this field of corn comprising nearly or quite fifty acres, was nicely harvested. I don't think ten bushels could have been saved from it.

RAINBOW BLUFF.

On the march at sunrise; just before noon we came out of the woods into an open country and in full view of the famous Rainbow bluff of which we had heard so much. The batteries were soon in position and skirmishers were sent out to examine the situation. After a time word came back that no enemy was near, the batteries lim'ered up and the march resumed. We were soon on the bluff, which was well fortified on the river and east sides but quite defenseless in the rear; it would have been an easy matter to have shelled out an enemy had there been one there. Here we found our gunboat fleet which had come up and was going to keep us company higher up the river. After destroying these works we moved on, reaching the little town of Hamilton about 2 p. m., and halted just outside. Here we were to stop three or four hours for rest and dinner.

A PRIVATE DINNER PARTY.

I suggested to Doctor Ben that it would be a good plan to forage our dinner; to this he assented and said if I could find some sweet potatoes he would furnish the chicken or pig. We started out, going up town; here we separated, each one to obtain his share of the dinner and then meet again on the corner. I was not long in finding a garden in which grew the potatoes; making a break in the fence I soon filled my haversack, and returning to the corner, waited for the doctor. Great was my surprise to soon see him coming down the street with a hen dangling by the legs, and in charge of an officer of the guard, going in the direction of the general's headquarters, on the veranda of which he and his staff were sitting. Being an interested party, I thought I would attend the conference. The officer preferred his charges, and Capt. Dim, the provost marshal, commenced the trial. He did not seem to get very much interested in it, and the doctor was getting along nicely with it, until the general began a cross examination by asking him if he had not heard the order in regard to foraging? The doctor admitted that he had. "How then does it happen that you do not observe it?" This was a pretty close question and I began to tremble for him, but he proved equal to the emergency; after waiting a moment he looked up and said, "General, this rebellion has got to be crushed if it takes every hen in North Carolina." A smile lit up the face of the general, who asked, "Where is your regiment?" "Just beyond here, sir." "Go to it, my boy, and get your dinner and be ready to march in a couple of hours or so." We started, congratulating each other over the fortunate turn affairs had taken. We had a good dinner, and were well rested when the order came to march, about 6 p. m.

BURNING OF HAMILTON.

This was a small town about half as large as Williamston, and like all other southern towns I have seen was built all in a heap. The inhabitants all left on our approach, and exhibited a bad feeling by cutting their well ropes and filling the wells with rubbish. This so incensed the boys that on leaving they set the town on fire, and we marched away by the light of it. A tramp of five or six miles up the Weldon road brought us to a plantation on which was a big cornfield. Into this we filed and put up for the night. Here again was forage for the team and cavalry horses and material for beds and fires. Our force of darkies was greatly augmented, they came in by hundreds, and after we had our supper the plantation dance was in order.

THE GUNBOATS THUNDERING UP THE RIVER.

The gunboats had come up the river, and were now working their way towards Halifax, causing, I presume, the people of that town a terrible fright. They would fire an occasional shot as an advance notice of their coming, and on the still night air the boom of the big guns far up the river was wafted back to our camp.

NOT SEEKING A FIGHT.

They were expecting us at Halifax and Weldon and were making preparations to receive us, but the general was not up in that part of the country looking for a fight. A battle up there would have been without results to us, unless it was the loss of men. He was up there simply looking over the country, picking up a few horses and mules and helping the planters do their harvesting. The general, not caring to go where they were expecting him, the next morning turned his course across the country towards Tarboro, a town on the Tar river, some twenty miles west, hoping to reach there before the enemy could concentrate their forces against him.

A RICH COUNTRY.

This day's march was through a rich and fertile section of country, abounding in large, rich plantations, affording plenty of luxuries for the boys and a great many horses and mules for the use of the army. The contrabands flocked in droves to our standard, and were very useful in carrying our blankets, filling canteens, foraging chickens and pigs, toting rails for the fires, and in many other ways. We harvested a large field of corn at noon and burned several barnfuls during the day, reaching camp late in the evening, some five or six miles from Tarboro. A heavy northeast rain storm set in during the night, and we could hear the cars running, bringing troops into Tarboro. Scouting parties were sent out to reconnoitre the enemy's force and position, and reported they were in force and fortified between us and the town. As the general's errand up through this part of the country was more for observation than fight, he thought with his small force of infantry (and a part of that new troops) and with a cumbersome wagon train, he had better act on the defensive, and early the next morning ordered a retreat.

THE RETREAT.

The morning was dark and dreary. With a heavy northeast rain storm blowing, the enemy in force in front of us and expecting an attack on our rear, when the retreat commenced our prospects were anything but flattering. Quietly the order was given for the wagons to start and make the time as short as possible back some eight miles to an old church and cross roads, past which we had come the day before, and there await further orders. Three companies of cavalry preceded us as an advance guard. The road was very muddy and the traveling hard, but that made no difference; the teams were urged forward and the boys exhibited remarkable enterprise in getting over the road. I thought I had never seen our boys more interested in anything than they were in this. Not even applejack nor all the luxuries that lay scattered along their pathway had any charms for them. Their whole souls seemed centered on the old church, and they were thoroughly absorbed in their efforts to reach it. I don't believe they ever took half so much interest before in going to a church. The old church and cross roads were reached before noon, and we anxiously awaited the arrival of the general. Not hearing any firing in the rear we concluded they were lying for us at some other point, if they were intending an attack on us. The cavalry informed us that the bridge across the creek out in the swamp, over which we crossed the day before, was taken up and things looked as though somebody might be waiting for us on the other side. The troops were now coming up, and a couple of batteries dashed past us, down the road into the swamp. The general soon came up and seemed quite pleased that he had gained this point without opposition, and thought there would be no further trouble.

The commander is a practical engineer, and can map with his eye the country as he passes through it, picking out the strong and weak positions, moving his troops in this or the other direction, holding such roads and positions as he thinks will give him an advantage, and when a movement is ordered, it is entered on by his troops with full confidence of success. Two roads branched from the one we were on, one taking a north-easterly direction, the other a north-westerly. Up these roads the cavalry were sent to make a reconnoissance. The pioneer corps was ordered down to the creek, over which the bridge had been taken up, and commenced felling trees as though they intended to rebuild it. After an hour's ride, the cavalry returned and reported everything all right. A part of the infantry and artillery now took the advance, going up the north-easterly road, followed by the wagon train, while the balance of the troops brought up the rear. While this was going on, the sharp ring of the axes could be heard out in the swamp as though that was the intended route, but after the column had got well under way, the pioneers abandoned their job and followed along. The route lay through an open country, easy of defence, and if anybody was waiting for us on the other side of the swamp (as we have since learned there was), they got nicely fooled. About night we reached the site where two days before stood the town of Hamilton. Nothing remained but a few scattered rookeries on the outskirts occupied by negroes. There was, however, one small two-story building standing a little apart from the others, which was saved, and into this went company B, taking the up-stairs tenement, while the lower one was occupied by a company of the 5th Massachusetts. The night was cold and stormy, snowing quite heavily, and the little army was obliged to stand it or find shelter as best they could. I reckon the boys who set the fires bitterly repented of their acts, as they must have suffered much, and a good many of them were worn down and sick from the long march.

By morning the storm had abated, but there were about two inches of soft snow or slush, and some of the boys were barefoot, having worn out their shoes, and a good many were nearly or quite sick. The surgeons looked over their regiments, sending the sick and bare-footed aboard the gunboats for Plymouth, for which place the troops were bound.

The order of exercises for today was a march back to Williamston, which I very much regretted not being able to do, as I rather enjoy these rambles through the country and feel disappointed when I cannot go, but I had been a little under the weather for a day or two, and was sent with the others aboard the little gunboat Hetzel, where we were greatly sympathized with by the marines, who seemed to think we had had a pretty hard time of it, and who showed us every favor and indulgence that lay in their power. The boats steamed slowly down the river, keeping along with the army, and arriving at Plymouth on the afternoon of the 10th, having made a two weeks' excursion.

THE RESULT.

I reckon the landed nobility up the country through which we traveled will never care to see another excursion of the same kind. They probably by this time begin to think that war is not so pretty a pastime, and the Confederate commissariat can mourn the loss of many thousand bushels of corn. We made a desolation of the country through which we passed, and that proud aristocracy can now look over their desolate fields, and in vain call the roll of their slaves; can sit down and make a nice calculation of how much better off they are under their Confederacy than they would have been had they remained loyal to the old flag. We cleaned up pretty much everything there was, bringing back with us upwards of 1000 negroes and several hundred horses and mules.

Coming down the river we ran past what appeared to be a large cotton plantation, when some 40 or 50 negroes came running down to the shore and begged to be taken aboard. They were the most forlorn and wretched looking beings I had ever seen; their clothing was little else than rags, scarcely covering their nakedness. Some of them followed us nearly a mile down the river, begging piteously to be taken aboard. I pitied the poor creatures, but was powerless to help them, and the thought occurred to me that if God cares for all his creatures, he surely must have forgotten these.

WE STAY AWHILE IN PLYMOUTH.

Nov. 20. All the troops, with the batteries, wagons, horses, mules and negroes, have been sent around to Newbern by boats, and we alone are left to garrison the town till further orders. In the meantime it would be agreeable to have a change of clothing. When we left Newbern, we left behind us our traveling satchels, with all our best clothes, taking nothing except what we had on, which is now in a very dirty and dilapidated condition with no chance to get any. The major seems to take a great pride in his regiment, but I really cannot see why he should take much in such a ragged, dirty, lousy set of vagabonds as we are, but anyway he does, and naturally likes to take us out for dress parade and show us up to the naval officers, of whom there are quite a number stationed here. In this he sometimes gets a little set back, when about half the boys appear out without any shirts on. At this he will mildly remonstrate, but will be told their shirts are out being washed, and they appear out with their blouses for shirts, with their pants and suspenders outside. This thing continued for a few nights, until the major became so disgusted he swore a big swear that he wouldn't have another dress parade until we had some shirts. That of course made the boys feel proper bad, and they said if that was the case, they would vote never to have any. Plymouth is a small but rather pretty town, situated on the south bank of the Roanoke river, about five miles up from the sound. It is a half shire town of Washington county, and contains two churches, two hotels, U. S. custom house, court house and jail, but no school-house. It has been a place of considerable trade, doing a good coasting business and exporting large quantities of cotton, corn, shingles, lumber, fish and naval stores. There are some Union people about here, who appear to be nice sort of folks, but nearly all of secesh proclivities are away.

WE LEAVE PLYMOUTH.

DEC. 24. On the 8th of December the regiment embarked on the schooner Skirmisher for Newbern, arriving there on the evening of the 10th. We were right glad to once more get back to camp, where we could clean ourselves up and get a change of clothing, but were much more glad to find mail and express matter from home. We were not, however, overjoyed to find an order awaiting us to be ready early in the morning to start on a long and rapid march, but having become accustomed to adapting ourselves to circumstances, the order was soon forgotten and we were absorbed in our letters and papers, after which the contents of the boxes were attended to. There was a generous quantity of goodies from the loved ones at home, some of which are of a perishable nature; what shall we do with them? We go off in the morning, and the Lord knows when we shall come back if we ever do. There are no taps tonight, and the candles burn long and well, so we sit down and gorge ourselves until we can eat no more, putting aside what we think will keep until we get back, and crowding as much as we can that remains into our haversacks. We next attend to a change of clothing, and by morning are ready for a start. I wear my best clothes, thinking if I should happen to become a guest at the Hotel de Libby, I should like to appear respectable.

GOLDSBORO EXPEDITION.

During our stay at Plymouth, large reinforcements of troops arrived at Newbern. These troops consisted of Gen. Wessell's brigade of six regiments of New York and Pennsylvania troops, and the 8th, 43d, 45th, 46th and 51st Massachusetts regiments of nine months' troops. They were to join in an expedition under Gen. Foster, against Goldsboro and the Wilmington and Weldon railroad; the object being to destroy that road, thus preventing reinforcements reaching Gen. Lee at Fredericksburg, where Gen.

Burnside was about making an assault. This part of the plan was successfully carried out, but too late to be of any use to Burnside, as he made his attack three days before we reached and destroyed the road. Although Gen. Foster started the moment his troops arrived, it was about a week too late.

The division consisted of four brigades, the 1st under command of Brig. Gen. Wessell; the 2d, Col. Amory; 3d, Col. Stevenson; 4th, Col. Lee; with the 3d New York cavalry and eleven batteries of artillery, and the wagon and ambulance train. The whole made a force of about 20,000 men, and when the procession was in line of march it covered a distance of about seven miles. Col. Heckman, with his 9th New Jersey regiment, was a kind of independent corps, he taking the contract to lead the advance and clear the way. The expedition started on the morning of Dec. 11, and about noon Col. Lee's brigade fell in on the left, the 25th being in this brigade and 18th regiment in the column. We marched this day about 12 miles, getting into camp late in the evening. This bivouac was on an extensive plain, and was covered with troops, horses, mules and wagons, and in the dim moonlight, its thousand camp fires made a grand illumination. It was not long after supper before the men were all rolled up in their blankets asleep, and on that cold December night, as I looked over that field and saw by the glare of its many camp fires, those thousands of brave, self-sacrificing men lie stretched upon the ground, I could but think that the bright spirits of the immortal band of American patriots hovered over that camp and looked down approvingly upon our efforts to sustain that government and these institutions for which they had sacrificed and suffered so much to establish.

On the morning of the 12th the march was resumed, but was necessarily slow as the roads were badly obstructed. In one swamp, for a distance of three miles, the trees were thickly felled across the road, making a forenoon's job for Capt. Wilson and his pioneer corps to clear away. They had no sooner finished this job when another presented itself in building a bridge across a creek, which took nearly all the afternoon. The 25th crossed this bridge about dark, and a little farther on saw lights ahead. We now thought we were nearing camp and we began to cheer up, thinking our day's work nearly over, but on coming to the camp fires, we found only the 51st Massachusetts, Col. Sprague, and a battery left here at the junction of the main road leading to Kinston, with orders to hold it until noon the next day, while the column moved up the old or back road towards Southwest creek. Finding this was not our hotel we took fresh courage and pushed on. A few miles farther brought us into camp. It was a cold night, and being nearly the last in we found the rails and wood had all been appropriated; we must either go without fires or go half a mile for fuel. We went for it, and after a hard scramble succeeded in getting a partial supply, enough however, with prudence, to go through the night and make our morning's coffee. Our march this day was only about ten miles.

Next morning we took an early start. A mile or two up the road, another road branched to the right, leading to Kinston. Here the 46th Massachusetts, Col. Shurtliff, with a battery were left to hold it. About the middle of the forenoon firing was heard in the advance; Col. Heckman had got a job. He found the enemy in considerable force at Southwest creek, and with his own and one or two other regiments succeeded in driving them out, capturing one gun. This Southwest creek, like all other battle grounds the enemy selects, is a swamp about half a mile wide, with a small creek running through it. We halted early in the afternoon, to let the teams, which were stuck all along the road, come up. We were now about five miles from Kinston. The infantry bivouacked on the left side of the road, on which was a growth of small pines, making a nice, clean camp-ground. The batteries and teams, as fast as they came up, were parked in the open field on the right. The cavalry, which we had not seen for two days, were playing a lone hand, and were scouting around over the country, making feints and bothering the enemy. Under the pines we make soft beds, and at dark kindle the fires, make coffee, eat our suppers and go to bed, expecting in the morning our further progress up the country will be vigorously disputed.

All was quiet during the night, and early in the morning of Sunday, the 14th, the camp was astir. The general ordered that in order to lighten the teams, every man take three days' rations and 60 rounds of extra ammunition. While this was being dealt out, some one suggested that the teams could be still further lightened by issuing a ration of whiskey. Acting on that suggestion, the liquor was ordered, and there was far less complaint about taking it than there was in taking the extra ammunition. Breakfast over, the chaplain offered prayer, after which a hymn was sung; we then filed into the road and commenced the march. The advance was well up the road, and we began to hear firing ahead. As we drew nearer it became more distinct and there was more of it. Wessell's and Amory's brigades were hotly engaged, and the roar of artillery gave notice that the batteries were not silent spectators.

We hurried on and soon met the stretcher corps bringing out the dead and wounded men. This to me was a sickening sight, to see men with pallid faces, writhing with pain and blood dripping from the stretchers. I know not how it is with others, but there is nothing that so completely takes the pith out of me when going into action as this. I want to get engaged before seeing the dead or wounded; after that I do not mind so much about it.

The enemy, under command of Gen. Evans, was in strong

force and posted on the south side of the river near Kinston, commanding the road that led through a thick, wet swamp some half a mile wide. This swamp prevented our batteries from working with much accuracy, consequently the fight became an infantry one. Wessell's and Amory's brigades pushed into the swamp and engaged them in front, while the other regiments as they came up were posted on the right, to prevent a flank movement, or to make one ourselves if necessary. The 25th, with Morrison's battery, were drawn up in line of battle on an open field near the river, to the left of the swamp. As the battle was confined to the swamp in front, we were not under fire at all. The battle lasted about three hours, when our troops got through the swamp and charged on them. The 9th New Jersey led the charge, followed by Wessell's and Stevenson's brigades. They charged them across the river and through the town, capturing eleven pieces of artillery and 300 prisoners. After which they shelled them, driving them up the country, out of sight and hearing. In this battle the enemy numbered about 8000, with several batteries of artillery. We had no means of knowing their loss, but it must have been considerable; they got off most of their wounded and probably some of their dead.

When Lee's brigade got on the battle-ground, it was halted, and burying parties were detailed to bury the enemy's dead which here covered the ground. This ground was hard and considerably higher than the swamp; in the midst of a pretty grove of trees stood an old church. The boys did not take very kindly to this burying business, as they were in a hurry to get into town and secure their share of the spoils, but the job had to be done, and they went about it with a will. They dug trenches a little more than two feet deep, and in these the dead were placed, with the capes of their overcoats wound around their heads; over those not having overcoats, pine boughs were thrown and all were covered over with earth. Our loss in this battle was about 200, some 50 of whom were killed, the 45th Massachusetts sharing largely in the loss. About dark we marched into a field a short distance south of the town, where we were to bivouac. Now commenced the destruction of fences and old buildings for fires, and after supper parties went up town to look over the prize, and late in the evening began to return bringing in their plunder. One party had been very successful; they came in hauling an express wagon loaded with tobacco, cigars, apple-jack, scuppernong wine, pigs, etc. Of course a dividend was struck, and all that wanted, had a share in the tobacco and cigars, with a drink or two of the wine and apple-jack. This was a pretty good Sunday's job.

Next morning, the 15th, the division was again on the move, destroying the road and railroad bridges over the Neuse river as we left. We marched up the river road about 18 miles, getting into camp late in the evening, having met with no obstacles dur ing the day. Here again was a scramble for rails and wood for fires; all the rails near by were gone, and we had to tote ours about a quarter of a mile. The fires kindled, making coffee was in order; after a twenty mile tramp and toting rails for fires, as they stood around them, roasting one side and freezing the other, the boys are not feeling very amiable. If there is any one thing more than another that will draw the cuss-words out of them, it is when a dozen cups of coffee are sitting along a burning rail boiling, and some careless fellow comes along, hits the end of the rail, dumping it all over. It is not the loss of the coffee they care so much about, but it is going perhaps half a mile for water to make more. It is of no sort of use to send a darky for it in the night, as he would not find his way back before morning.

On the morning of the 16th it was reported the enemy were in force across the river at a place called Whitehall, about three or four miles from where we were, and where they were building a steam ram. Of course that must be attended to, and when we left our bivouac, the ball had opened and heavy firing was heard ahead. Lee's brigade hurried on and an hour's march brought us to the scene of conflict. A road turned to the right, leading down to the river, where our batteries were at work. The 25th was ordered down this road, but when about half way down, and only a short distance in rear of the batteries, were ordered to halt and wait further orders. An artillery duel was being fought, our batteries on the south side of the river and the enemy's on the north, with the bridge up that here crossed the river. We had ten batteries engaged, and the enemy had what we had not captured at Kinston. The roar of artillery, screaming shot and bursting shell was fearful. The enemy had sharpshooters along the river bank, who were rather troublesome to our artillerists, and to meet them men were called for from our regiments; Major Pickett was called on for 100. He asked for volunteers and more than half the regiment stepped forward for the service. I didn't volunteer; I never do; I rather pride myself on not committing a great amount of foolishness in this business. The 100 were soon off for the river, where they took available positions and did good service. In this engagement they had one killed and three wounded. After nearly three hours the fire began to slacken and the enemy drew off. The steam ram on the river, which was said to be quite a formidable craft, was then blown up and destroyed. It will be rather discouraging to attempt the building of any more rams at this navy-yard. The army then moved up the road, getting into camp about night, and some seven or eight miles from Goldsboro. Early in the morning of the 17th, Lee's brigade took the advance, and after a march of five or six miles, the scouts reported the enemy in the woods near the railroad and bridge which crosses the river about two miles below

Goldsboro. We were now in their immediate neighborhood. The column was halted, a regiment sent out as skirmishers and a battery advanced and took position on a knoll of ground, a little to the left and front of the column, and commenced shelling the woods. This had the effect of stirring them up, so we knew where they were. The infantry and batteries were ordered forward, and marched into position in front of the enemy, covering the railroad and bridge. After some skirmishing, at about 10 a. m., the battle commenced and continued with short intermissions until the middle of the afternoon, at which time we had silenced the enemy's guns and driven them from the field. We burned the railroad bridge, and with the help of the cavalry tore up and burned ten or twelve miles of track and tressel work of the Wilmington and Weldon railroad. Gen. Foster then said the object had been accomplished, and ordered a retreat, Lee's brigade being ordered to cover it. It was near sunset when we left the field. Morrison's New York and Belger's Rhode Island batteries alone remaining on a knoll of ground which they had occupied during the battle, waiting for us to get away, when they would follow. After leaving the field, we crossed the bed of a small creek about 20 feet wide, with scarcely any water, but with steep banks, except at the ford, where they sloped down to admit crossing.

Crossing this creek, we halted at a farm house a little way off to load our dead and wounded men into ambulances. While doing it a battery officer dashed up exclaiming, "For God's sake, send us an old regiment! The enemy are charging our batteries! Quick! hurry up!" The 27th and 25th Massachusetts were on the left or rear of the column, and immediately faced about and started on the double quick for the batteries. In the meantime, while our troops were leaving the field, the enemy had been reinforced, and, seeing the batteries alone, and perhaps thinking they might be out of ammunition, thought it would be a nice little trick to capture them. In going to the relief of the batteries we had to run a gauntlet of shot and shell from a six-pounder battery out in the woods, a little to the left and front of our batteries, who were supporting their charging brigade. We went to Belger's support, and the 27th to Morrisson's. In the meantime the batteries had opened fire on the charging columns but without checking them. When we came up they were coming across the railroad; but another discharge from the guns, and seeing their support, the enemy thought they had taken too much of a job, and facing about they put for the woods.

That little battery out in the woods was wonderfully active, shying their shot and shell thick and fast. Fortunately their guns had a high elevation, and the shot went several feet above our heads. They soon corrected that, however, and the shot began to come lower. Capt. Belger ordered us to lie down, I am always quick to hear that order, and was the first man down. They had now got their range well down, the shot just skimming over us, one shell had burst in front of us, killing one man and wounding two others. They had a splendid range on me as I lay in the rear of my company. About once a minute a shot would come directly over me, striking the ground only a few feet in the rear, and what made it more provoking, they kept getting them lower, until I had flatted out as thin as a sheet of tissue paper. I could stand this no longer, and told the boys in front of me that those shot were coming dangerously close, and they had better make a break by crowding a little to the right and left. I pushed along about ten feet to the left and would liked to have pushed about ten miles to the rear. That movement was barely executed when a shot ploughed a furrow through the space they had made. But that was their last shot, for after the charging column had turned, the guns were turned on that battery, and annihilated it at the first discharge, or at least, I supposed that was the case, as we heard nothing more from it. It was now after sunset and peace once more reigned in Warsaw.

We waited awhile to see if they wanted anything more of us, and finding they did not, we again drew off the field. On coming to the little creek, which we had crossed dry shod an hour before, we now found a roaring torrent running bankfull, with barrels, rails and pieces of timber borne on the surface of its swift current. We had got to go through it, and the boys, holding their rifles, cartridge boxes and blankets above their heads, waded in. The water was waist deep, and when my company went in I waited on the bank, thinking I would step into the rear as they passed by, but I made a wrong calculation of the bank. When I stepped in, I went in all over, and in trying to recover myself, I let go my cartridge box, blanket and Spitfire, but caught the last between my knees, and commenced ducking to get it. The major was standing on the bank, cautioning the boys to keep their powder dry. When he happened to observe me going through my aquatic performances he yelled vociferously: "What in hell are you doing there? Why don't you keep your powder up out of the water?" I paid no attention to him, but kept reaching for Spitfire, and every time I reached for it, the current would nearly take me off my feet. After I had succeeded in fishing it out, I turned my attention to the major, and answered his little conundrum by asking him what in hell powder was good for without Spitfire? The major laughed and jumping on a gun carriage was ferried across. I was a little the worst off of the lot for I was thoroughly soaked, as were also all my belongings.

The night was freezing cold and in our wet clothes we felt it very sensibly. A mile march brought us to the woods, which were some four or five miles through, and on the other side was our last night's bivouac. The advance troops had set the woods on fire and when we went through, it was a roaring mass of flame.

This served us a good turn, as it lighted up the road and kept us warm. We reached our bivouac late in the evening, wet, cold, tired and hungry, but our day's work was not yet done. If we wanted fires and hot coffee, we must go half a mile for rails and tote them in on our shoulders. We brought in a good supply and soon had our coffee boiling. Our wagons were bare of meat and whiskey, and our supper consisted of coffee and hardtack.

Through the long, weary night, wet, cold and hungry, we stood shivering over the fires. Gladly we hailed the first grey streaks of dawn and took fresh courage, knowing we should soon be on the road for home. At sunrise the whole army was in motion, on the road for Newbern, where we arrived a little after noon on Sunday, the 21st, nearly dying from hunger and exhaustion.

When we started on this expedition it was thought the wagons contained an ample supply of rations, but our march up the country was so impeded by blockaded roads and so vigorously contested that it was prolonged beyond what was anticipated; besides it was an awful poor section of country for pigs, chickens and apple-jack. On this little excursion, Gen. Foster's army has been out ten days, marching 150 miles, cutting out several miles of blockaded roads, building one bridge, doing considerable skirmishing, whipping the enemy three times on their own ground, besides other mischief, such as burning the railroad bridge at Goldsboro, burning a train of cars and smashing up an engine at Mount Olive station, some ten miles down the road from the battle ground, and also tearing up the track between the two points. This last deviltry the 3d New York cavalry is accountable for. There was also burned a quantity of cotton, several houses, barns and many thousands of dollars' worth of fencing and timber. A very clever little job for one trip, but the results would have been greater had it been done two weeks sooner; it would then have greatly hindered the reinforcing of Gen. Lee at Fredericksburg. However, there can no blame be laid to Gen. Foster, as he started on the execution of his orders as soon as the troops arrived.

MAJOR PICKETT.

Our little major since the two last tramps has become very popular in his regiment, and I expect when the eagles light on his shoulders we shall feel pretty proud of him. He is a staving good fellow, and in a fight is always on the lead, inspiring the men with courage by his coolness and daring. On the road he is equally good, letting the boys have it pretty much their own way, never troubling himself about how they came by their chickens and apple-jack, and is often seen trudging along on foot, letting some sick or footsore soldier ride his giraffe.

CHAPTER V.

THE NEW YEAR.

JANUARY 1, 1863. By the blessing of God we have entered the portals of another year. Who knows what storms within it hide? Who can tell how many of us will enter on another year? but let us not despond; let us look with bright hopes to the future, going manfully forward, overcoming all obstacles in our path. We know the hardships, privations and dangers through which we have passed the last year, perils by sea and perils by land, meeting death in a thousand forms, but by an unseen hand have been brought safely through. It has now been fifteen months since our regiment was organized, and we then thought that by this time the trouble would be over and the rebellion would have become a thing of the past. But not so; it seems to have taken deeper root and there is no telling when it will end. It is true our armies have met with many successes and have also met with some reverses; the army of the Potomac has met with nothing but disaster from the first and will probably meet with nothing else until let alone by the war office at Washington. The enemy has a number of cruisers afloat making havoc with our merchant marine, and every success of their army inspires them with fresh hope and courage. I am reminded of what my new-found friend here in town told me a few days after we came here, that I would, if nothing happened to me, serve out my three years and could then re-enlist. I thought then the man was crazy, now I am not quite sure but he was the better prophet of the two.

THE MAJOR'S EAGLES.

FEB. 1. At last the major's eagles, which have so long been winging their flight this way, have alighted on his shoulders, and he looks as pert and gamy as a wildcat. Bully boy! long may you wave! Promotions will now come along right smart, and I have no doubt I have been thought of for some important position, but I shall decline all promotions; I had rather be a door-keeper at the guardhouse than to dwell in the tents of wickedness.

WE LEAVE FOR PLYMOUTH.

NEWBERN, WEDNESDAY, MARCH 18. After months of idleness in camp, at last comes a change. At 4 o'clock p. m., orders came to break camp, pick up our traps and be ready to march in half an hour. Dark found seven companies of us on board the steamer Escort, bound for Plymouth. Companies A, E and H were left to follow on another boat. The night being dark and stormy we waited till morning before leaving.

MARCH 19. Heavy northeast storm blowing this morning. Steamer starts down the river and enters the sound about 10 o'clock, wind increases, the sound grows rough, the boat rolls, the boys grow sick, the water breaks on deck and many of them get wet; altogether the passage is rather unpleasant. We arrive at the north end of the sound, near the entrance to Croaton sound, about 9 p. m., and anchor for the night.

MARCH 20. This morning finds the storm unabated. The boat starts at daylight, passing Roanoke island, and enters the Albemarle, arriving at Plymouth late in the afternoon, where we make our quarters in a large warehouse on the wharf.

MARCH 22. The garrison here consists of companies G, Capt. Swift, and H. Capt. Sanford, of the 27th Massachusetts; company D, Capt. Howard, of the 5th Massachusetts: company C, Capt. Cliffton, of the 1st North Carolina Union volunteers, and part of a company of North Carolina cavalry. Several gunboats lying in the river. The fellows here are telling us bear stories about one rebel General Garnett (whoever he is) and his brigade which is hovering around here. I think he must be quite a harmless character to let so small a garrison as this go undisturbed, but it is possible he has a wholesome fear of Capt. Flusser and his gunboats. This town has undergone quite a change since we were here last fall. During the winter the enemy made a dash in here, setting the town on fire, burning up the central and business portion of it. These people have singular ideas; they seem to think that by destroying their property, they are in some way damaging us, but if we destroy any property it is a great piece of vandalism. I reckon they will sometime see their mistake and repent of it in dust and ashes.

GEN. FOSTER ARRIVES.

MARCH 24. Gen. Foster arrived this morning and went to work laying out a fort and other defences which we are to build. That job done, he took companies F, I and K of the 25th and H of the 27th Massachusetts with a party of marines, and a boat howitzer (on board his boat, the John Ferrin,) and left on some sort of an excursion up the Chowan river. The general is no idler, he is always on the move and seeing that everybody else is. He is ubiquitous, turning up at any time in all parts of his domain, and keeping everybody within fifty miles on the qui vive.

PITCHING CAMP.

MARCH 27. We have cleared off the debris from a portion of the burnt district and pitched our camp there. The colonel might take a little more pride in showing us up to the naval officers at dress parade than he did when we were here last fall, but he is in command of the post; Lieut. Col. Moulton is in command of the regiment and he will do the honors. The 46th Massachusetts has arrived and will pitch their camp on the right of us, in the burnt district.

WORK ON THE FORT.

Work commenced today on the defences. Capt. Foster of Company D is to be superintendent and general boss. I was detailed to take command of a working party from my company. Now this was all new business to me. I knew nothing about building forts, so I stood with my men and looked on. This was not very hard work, but after a spell the captain said, "Bring your men this way." The order was promptly responded to, and the boys set to work. I thought they worked well enough, although I noticed that the bank in front of them did not rise very fast, but I supposed that was owing to the hardness of the soil. After a while they complained of feeling tired; I told them to rest, and they squatted. After that they seemed to be tired pretty much of the time. The captain would come along and ask me why my men were not working. I would answer him that they were tired, and after resting would handle their spades right smart. At night we had a bank thrown up about a rod long and nearly a foot high, but the boys worked well and I know they will sleep well after it.

Companies A, E and H arrived yesterday, and also the companies of the expedition who left with the general, except company I, which remains at Edenton for a few days.

CHURCH SERVICE.

MARCH 29. Church service today for the first time in several weeks; we occupied the Methodist church. Chaplain James discoursed on neutrality. He said there could be no such thing as neutrality; a man must be one thing or the other, and those who do not declare for the government, should be treated as its enemies. The house was well filled with soldiers and the galleries running around three sides of the house were filled with darkies, who somewhat resembled an approaching thunder squall.

PICKET DUTY.

APRIL 5. I fear I was not appreciated on the fort, as I was superseded after my first day's effort and have since been assigned to other duty; but I nobly served my country, and I know that history will do me justice. Yesterday I was out in the country among the wild flowers. I went out with a picket guard, about three miles in a southeasterly direction, to what is called Mills cross-roads, relieving the old picket. After spreading our blankets on the grass beside the fence, we entered vigorously on our duty of waiting and watching for the rebel Gen. Garnett, and listening to the sweet warbling of the singing birds. There is nothing in picket duty that stirs up a great amount of enthusiasm, but still it is a good steady business, with occasionally a little ray of excitement, as when a darky comes along and one has to examine his pass.

About the middle of the afternoon, we heard the approach of horses, and looking up the road, saw two ladies coming at a swift gallop towards us. My first impulse was to charge cavalry, but I refrained from doing so, as I saw they were not enemies. As they came up, I recognized Mesdames Bartholomew and Clifton. I turned out the guard and extended to them the customary civilities. They said they were out for an afternoon's ride and supposed it was as far as they could go in that direction. I told them they might go farther if they wished, and I should be pleased to furnish them an escort, only it would weaken my lines. They laughed and thanked me for my gallantry, but thought they had better not venture farther. I inquired if there were any news stirring in town, and they answered, "All quiet on the Roanoke." They then bade us good afternoon and started on the retreat. There is no church service today; all hands are busy at work on the fort, and things are beginning to look as though war was liable to break out at almost any time.

NEWS FROM ALONG THE LINE.

APRIL 10. The siege of Washington on the Pamlico river continues, and heavy firing is heard from there every day. We learn they have got Gen. Foster shut up there and he is in danger of being made prisoner. That may be, but I will bet ten to one he holds the keys and will never take off his cap to any general in the Confederate service.

APRIL 16. Work goes bravely on at the fort; one gun mounted today and if we can have two or three days more we shall be ready to receive company. Our little force here is being well handled, and with the aid of the boats can make a stubborn resistance. We heard that Gen. Spinola left Newbern with quite a force, going overland to the relief of Gen. Foster, but when about half way there he got scared and turned back. Gen. Foster will not compliment him very highly for that feat. I have heard a rumor that we have had an invitation to surrender; that a flag of truce came to our lines and requested an interview with the post commander. Col. Pickett went out. They said something about his surrendering, when the colonel replied he had not been in communication with his superior recently and had received no orders to surrender, and that under the circumstances he thought it wouldn't look hardly military to surrender without first burning a little powder over it. He then dismissed the flag. Bravo, colonel, bravo!

EVACUATION.

APRIL 19. The steamer Thomas Collyer arrived last night, bringing dispatches of some kind, but just what we were unable to find out. This morning, however, the mystery was cleared up. The 12th New York battery was on the wharf, the 46th Massachusetts and the other detached companies were breaking camp, preparatory to going aboard the boat. This meant evacuation and going to the relief of Foster. The 25th of course is to be the last to leave, and we cast the last sad, lingering look on Plymouth. That is always our style; the first in and last out, and never lost a battle. But just here, the uncertainty of all things human is again illustrated. Just as the troops were aboard, the old Massasoit comes puffing up the river, bringing the welcome news that Foster has run the blockade and the order of evacuation is countermanded. Cheer after cheer rends the air, smiles light up every countenance and hope takes the place of despair. But won't there be larks now, though? If there is anybody hanging around Washington who does not belong there, they had better be getting away.

COLONEL SISSON.

It seems that after Spinola's abortion and the troops' return to Newbern, the brave Col. Sisson of the 5th Rhode Island was so disgusted with the whole thing that he proposed going with his regiment alone to Foster's relief. He and his regiment went aboard the steamer Escort, and on the evening of the 13th, under cover of a heavy fire from the gunboats on the batteries at Hill's Point, seven miles below Washington, he successfully ran the blockade, arriving at Washington with his troops and supplies. The next evening, with Gen. Foster aboard, he again ran the gauntlet, landing the general safely in Newbern. But it is said the Escort looked like a pepper-box from the shot holes made in her while running the gauntlet. On this perilous trip only one man (the pilot) was killed. The little garrison at Washington held out bravely. It consisted of only eight companies of the 27th and the 44th Massachusetts regiments, two companies of the 1st North Carolina, one company of the 3d New York cavalry and one New York battery, aided by two or three gunboats on the river. Against this small force was opposed some 12,000 of the enemy as near as we can learn. After Gen. Foster got away they did not seem to care to wait for his return, but folded their tents and silently stole away.

ALL QUIET ON THE ROANOKE.

APRIL 24. The noise of the battle is over and we are no longer harassed by war's dread alarms, but can now sit down, eat our fresh shad and herring and drink our peach and honey in peace and quiet.

A BROKER'S OFFICE.

Our provost marshal, Major Bartholomew of the 27th Massachusetts, has opened a broker's office, where he is exchanging salt and amnesty for allegiance oaths, and as this is the fishing season, he is driving a right smart business. The natives for miles around come in droves, take the oath, get their amnesty papers and an order for salt, and after being cautioned not to be found breaking their allegiance they go away happy. There are probably some honest men among them who would like to do about right if they dared to, but the whole thing looks ludicrous, for there is evidently not one in a hundred of them who would ever think of taking the oath were it not for the hope of obtaining a little salt. The boys call it the salt oath.

A GOOD SENSIBLE TALK.

APRIL 28. I was out in the country yesterday, doing picket duty, and fell in with an old gentleman with whom I had a good sensible talk. He was an intelligent, well appearing man, who said he was a farmer, or had been one until the breaking out of the war. He owns a plantation just outside our lines, but is not permitted to go into town. He is allowed to purchase in small quantities such articles as he may need by sending in his negro man or getting the boys to bring them out. He said at the commencement of the secession movement, he and all this part of the state, in fact nearly all of the state, was opposed to it, and in two state conventions, to both of which he was a delegate, the ordinance of secession was rejected, and not until after South Carolina on one side and Virginia on the other had gone out was the ordinance of secession passed.

He said: "Situated as we were we could not remain neutral, and although opposed to it from the beginning and all the time even after the war commenced and all our young men had gone into the army, it was but natural that I should sympathize with my own people."

"Certainly," I replied, "but have you any hopes of the ultimate success of the Confederacy?"

"None whatever, and I told our people so at our conventions. We are a ruined people and the best thing we can do is to make peace with the government on any terms we can."

"Yes, but you know the terms are very simple, merely to lay down your arms and return to your loyalty to the government."

"Yes, I know it is simple enough now, but I reckon the government at Richmond is not wise enough to accept it, and the longer they keep up the war the worse we are off, and in the end we will have to accept such terms as are dictated to us."

A sensible old gentleman that, and I should have liked to go out to his place and sample his peach and honey, scuppernong and things.

MY DIARY. 91

STOKES TAKES HIS LEAVE OF US.

An order was received here today from the war department discharging Stokes from the service. When the order was read, it took him by surprise as it was his first intimation of it. He seemed disappointed and said he should like well enough to go home a few days, but did not like the idea of going to stay and thought he should be back with us again in a few weeks. He left for home this afternoon. I am sorry to lose Stokes and shall miss him very much. He was my chief of staff and I placed great reliance on him. He was one of our best boys, possessed of excellent judgment, and was unsurpassed in the secret service. I parted with him with many regrets and shall always retain pleasant memories of our soldier life.

WE RETURN TO NEWBERN.

MAY 3. Attended church this morning. Steamer Thomas Collyer arrived this afternoon with orders for the regiment to report at Newbern. All was bustle and hurrah boys; down came the tents and a general packing up followed. At dark we were aboard the boat, and, giving three cheers to Capt. Flusser and his men, steamed down the river. We had a beautiful moonlight night and a splendid sail down the Albemarle; arriving at Newbern in the afternoon of the 4th, we went into the Foster barracks for the night.

ON THE OLD CAMP GROUND.

MAY 5. This morning we pitched our tents once more on Camp Oliver. This seems like home again. We shall now have little else than guard duty to perform, keep ourselves slicked up and do the town. This is what we call being on waiting orders, but as the colonel has not had a hack at us lately, I presume he will want to practice some new evolutions he has been studying up out of the tactics. At any rate, we shall not long remain idle.

THE BOYS' STORY.

MAY 25. For the past day or two I have been a good deal amused and interested in hearing the boys relate their adventures at Dover and Gum swamps. Their stories conflict a little, but as near as I can make it out I fix up a little story: To prepare it a little, we hold an outpost and signal station some twelve miles up the railroad, at Bachellor's creek towards Kinston. This is garrisoned by the 58th Pennsylvania, Col. Jones. He is one of those stirring, active, restless sort of men, always finding out everything and getting interested in it. Well, he had discovered an outpost of the enemy some ten or twelve miles in his front and some six miles this side of Kinston, at a place called Gum swamp, and garrisoned by a considerable force. Now it occurred to him that it would be a capital joke to capture that post. So he comes down and shows his plans to the general, asking permission and troops to carry them out. He knew just who was there and how many; he had been around that swamp half a dozen times and knew all about it. That suited the general; he patted Jones on the back, called him a good fellow and told him to sail in, and he should have all the troops he wanted.

On the afternoon of the 21st, the 25th, with two or three other regiments, went aboard the cars for Bachellor's creek. Not feeling very well, I was excused from going. Arriving at the creek, Col. Jones with his regiment heads the column, and leads off into the woods. This was a night march, and just here I will explain that always on the march, whether day or night, all the officers that are mounted (and any of them can be who will take the trouble to steal an old horse or mule), have a disagreeable habit of riding up and down the column, opening it to the right and left, and those that have the least business do the most riding. The boys have become so accustomed to jumping out each side of the road on hearing Right and Left, that this is about the first thing they do on hearing almost any order.

THEY SEE A GHOST OR SOMETHING.

Sometime towards midnight the boys heard the cry, "Right and Left, double quick!" They made a jump, and just then what appeared to them like a streak of greased lightning went down the line. They say it wasn't a horse or man or anything they ever saw, and they are so filled with the marvelous and supernatural that some of them actually think they saw some sort of phantom or ghost. What they saw was probably a frightened deer or fox, but in the lone, dark woods, and near the witching hour of midnight, with their nerves and imaginations strained to their utmost tension, expecting that any moment, almost anything might happen, it is not surprising that they could see ghosts, phantoms and witches. But it is laughable to hear them tell it.

A COUNCIL OF WAR.

Soon after midnight they reached Core creek. Here they halted to rest and concert their plans. It was agreed that Jones, with his regiment and the 27th Massachusetts should make a detour around and gain the rear of the enemy, while the others were engaging their attention in front. When they heard him thundering in the rear, they were to charge in, and bag the whole swag. The plan was successfully carried out, so far as the charging in was concerned, but as they charged in most of the enemy charged out on either flank and escaped. They met with partial success, however, as they captured 165 prisoners, one 12-pounder gun, fifty horses and mules, and destroyed their camp and earthworks. The conflict was not very severe, as they had only five or six men slightly wounded. After having accomplished their object and sending off their trophies, instead of immediately starting on their return march, they lingered amid the scenes of their triumphs until late in the afternoon, when the enemy in force, swooped down upon them, cutting them off from the railroad and with shot and shell greatly accelerated their retreat.

THE RETREAT.

Late in the evening they reached Core creek, and being a little beyond pursuit, halted to rest. But instead of forcing the march and reaching our lines the same night, they crouched down and remained till morning. Then they discovered the enemy on three sides of them, with an almost impenetrable swamp on the other. This was Dover swamp, and as near as I can judge was similar to the one we went through on Roanoke island, only of greater extent. There was only one choice, and that must be quickly accepted. Into the swamp they plunged, with mud and water to their knees, and thick tangle brush and briars higher than their heads. They could go only in single file, and their progress was slow and tedious. Towards noon they were met by another enemy; the water in their canteens had given out and they began to experience an intolerable thirst. With a burning sun above them and scarcely a breath of air, with all manner of insects, reptiles and creeping things around them, their condition was indeed pitiable. Still they pressed forward, some of them filtering the slimy, muddy water through their caps or handkerchiefs and drinking it, but it served better as an emetic than for quenching thirst. About 2 p. m., they emerged from the swamp, and nearly dying from exhaustion, reached our lines at Bachellor's creek. Here they had rest and refreshment, after which they boarded the cars and arrived back to camp about night, tired, ragged, covered with mud and completely played out. This was their Gum swamp excursion as they tell it. After the boys had left for home, the enemy still hovered around the vicinity of Col. Jones' camp, and in his impulsive way he went out to meet them, and while skirmishing with them was shot dead. The enemy soon afterwards retired. Col. Jones was a brave man but of rather rash judgement.

HILL'S POINT.

JULY 3. Received orders for the right wing, consisting of companies K, I, F, C and B to break camp and be ready to march at an hour's notice. At noon the baggage was all on the wagons and we awaited orders. At 1 p. m., we were ordered into town, and companies F, C and B went aboard the little steamer Mystic, and companies K and I went aboard the Washington Irving, bound for Washington on the Pamlico river.

Left Newbern at 4 p. m., and had a fine sail down the river and through the sound, turning into the Pamlico about dark, and running up to within a few miles of Washington, where we anchored for the night. Early the next morning, we reached our destination. Soon after we were ordered back down the river, and companies K and I landed at Rodman's point, four miles below town, while the Mystic kept on and landed F, C and B at Hill's Point, three miles lower down, relieving a New York battery company which was on duty there.

Our first business was to tote our baggage and camp equipage up the bluff, and under a broiling sun we worked hard, at least I thought it was hard. I carried my knapsack up and was so exhausted I thought I had better celebrate the rest of the day. I started out to explore the surroundings, and soon my eye rested on a board shanty at the foot of the bluff. I entered and found a noble scion of African descent; he was running a restaurant, his whole stock consisting of corn meal, with which he made hoe cakes for the boys on the bluff. I inquired if he intended remaining here or going with the company we had just relieved. He said he should stay if he met with sufficient encouragement from the boys. I gave him a great deal of encouragement, telling him I thought he would have right smart of business and would do well, that I would give him my patronage and that he might commence now by making me one of his best hoecakes for dinner. He said it would be ready in half an hour. I went out and worked hard during that time, watching the boys get the freight up the bluff. I went for the cake and was shown one about fifteen inches across and of good thickness. I began mentally to size my pile, thinking I had been a little indiscreet. I inquired the price of that monstrosity, and was told it was ten cents. I felt relieved and handing out the dime, took the cake and went up the bluff. Here I met Spencer and asked him if he had any meat. He replied, "just a little." I showed him the hoe cake and said I thought we had better dine together; he thought so, too. Getting a cup of water, we sat down on a log and ate our Fourth of July dinner. The afternoon was used up in pitching tents and mounting picket guard. Thus was spent the Fourth of July, 1863.

SUNDAY, JULY 5. Like most other Sabbaths in the army, so was this; all day busy cleaning up the camp ground, tearing down the board shanties which former occupants had erected and using the material for flooring in our tents. We had our Fourth of July dinner today; bean soup, hoe cake and lemonade. Hill's Point is not a point in the river, as the stream here runs straight, but is a bluff some 25 feet higher than the river and about 20 rods wide. It is the terminus of the table-land beyond, and is formed by wide, deep ravines on either side which run back and soon ascend to the level of the table-land. Heretofore the enemy had a habit of running batteries down here and intercepting the boats coming up the river, forming a sort of blockade, causing our gunboats to waste right smart of ammunition, or necessitating the marching of troops across the country from Newbern to drive them out. During the siege last spring, they had a powerful battery here which caused Gen. Foster a heap of trouble. Since then he has occupied it himself. This is an intrenched camp, sporting three brass six-pounder field pieces. When or by whom these works were built is to me unknown, but they look like the work of the enemy. They contain a great number of angles; commencing on the edge of the bluff next the river, they run several rods along the edge of the ravines, then cross in front of the camp, and from any part of the line can be got direct, cross and enfilading fires. The three guns are in battery on the flanks and center. Major Atwood is in command, and in his absence, Capt. Foss of company F. Such is a description of our present abiding place.

I GET PROMOTED.

JULY 7. Today a sergeant, corporal and eight privates from each company have been detailed to manipulate the big guns. I had the honor of being selected from my company, and was assigned the left gun, a most dangerous and hazardous position. I feel proud of my promotion and am sure I shall sustain the honor of the artillery service. For a day or two we shall be under the instructions of a battery sergeant who will instruct us in loadings and firings. We shall also have to inform ourselves from a small book, giving instruction in loading and firing, and in calculating distances, elevations and depressions of the guns. My gun on the left occupies a very commanding position, being some ten feet higher than the other guns. From the top of the parapet to the bottom of the ravine, it is some 30 or 40 feet, and a part of the way nearly perpendicular. I have a range of the whole clearing and covering both the other guns; because of its great natural strength and commanding position, I have dubbed it the Malakoff. I being the senior sergeant, am styled on all hands, by both officers and men, as the chief of artillery, a rank I accept and have assumed all the privileges which that rank implies.

The little steamer Undine plies between town and this port, making her trips mornings and afternoons, giving us frequent and easy transit to town. I intend giving my command two or three passes a day, so they can visit town if they wish to. I am going to be liberal with them, and then if their professional services should be required, I shall expect them to stand by those guns and fight like bloodhounds till the last armed foe expires.

WHISKEY RATIONS.

JULY 10. This being an isolated post and several miles from any commissary or sutler, the officers feared it would be terribly infected with malaria; having regard for the health and welfare of the men, they prevailed on our assistant surgeon, Doctor

Flagg, to order whiskey rations. Up went the order and down came the whiskey, and now the order is to drink no more river water, but take a little whiskey as a preventive. This will prove a terrible hardship to the boys, but the surgeon's orders are imperative. The boys in camp get their whiskey at night, and the pickets in the morning when they come in. After a barrel of whiskey has stood out all day in the sun and got about milk warm, it is curious to observe the boys while drinking it. Some of them with rather tender gullets will make up all manner of contortions of face trying to swallow it, but will manage to get it down and then run about fifteen rods to catch their breath. Commanders of companies deal out the whiskey to their men, consequently I deal out to mine, and when I wish to reward any of my braves for gallant and meritorious conduct, I manage to slop a little extra into their cups. That keeps them vigilant and interested and gallant. Meritorious conduct consists in bringing in watermelons, peaches and other subsistence, of which they *somehow* become possessed.

A CONFLICT OF AUTHORITY.

JULY 20. There is among army officers a constant jealousy and strife for promotion and rank, watching and looking after each other, fearful lest some one may be assuming some rank or taking some privileges that do not belong to him. I have been giving my men passes out of camp, and these passes have been honored at headquarters. In consequence of that a spirit of envy and jealousy entered the breasts of the infantry officers; it made them feel sore and uneasy, so they consulted together and decided that that could no longer be allowed. They informed me that I was exceeding my authority in passing men out of camp. Being in a minority and not caring to exhibit any stubbornness over so trifling a matter I magnanimously waived my authority to issue the passes, but it was a big come down for the chief of artillery. When I wish to leave I simply look in at headquarters and say to the captain, "I propose going out." If there is anything in the *pitcher* he always says, "You had better come in, and take something before going." The captain is as generous as he is brave, and brave men are always generous.

A FIELD DAY.

AUGUST 1. We had been drilling and going through the motions of artillery firing every day for a month, and a few days ago it was thought best to test our theory by a little practice. Each gun was to fire eight rounds. The targets, about the size of a large barn, were set up 600 yards in front of the guns.

At noon the pickets were called in from out the woods and soon after the firing commenced. I ordered a blank to commence with to see if the old gun would shoot. It spoke out splendidly;

I was pleased with it; I then ordered a solid shot. It was fired and went somewhere, I don't know where; but it didn't hit the target. Calculating that a shell will travel a mile in seven seconds and the target was about a third of a mile away, I thought I would try one with the fuse at three seconds. It was fired and burst at the muzzle of the gun. That was not satisfactory. I then ordered another with the fuse at five seconds. This exploded when about half way to the target. I began to think those shell were all intended for short range anyway, and ordered one at one second. It was fired, and I heard it whizzing off through the woods a mile away. I was disgusted with shell practice and thought I would try canister. We fired one and I could see the bushes cut away at about 200 yards. Those shots had been fired at two degrees elevation. I ordered the corporal to sight the gun at the tops of the trees out in the woods, and tried another canister. This was better, the shot scattering about the target. We had now only one more shot, I thought I would try a solid one, and ordered the gun sighted at the top of the target. This was an excellent shot and I know it must have gone very near the target as I saw the top of a tree shake out in the woods in a direct line of the target.

On the whole, the firing was not entirely satisfactory, but the gunnery was all that could be desired and I am inclined to think the fault was in the ammunition. I think it must have been shopworn or second-hand. But perhaps I ought not to find too much fault, as this was our first practice. I am now impatient for an attack, for I know we can hold this post against any force that would be likely to be brought against it, and demonstrate to the country that we are heroes descended from heroes.

AN INSPECTION.

August 12. A few days ago orders came to get ready for inspection the next afternoon. All was now hurry and bustle, cleaning up camp, arms, equipments and clothing, and putting everything in order. The artillerists worked like beavers, cleaning up the gun carriages and limbers, using all the grease in the kitchen to brighten them up. The old brass guns were polished up and shone like mirrors and we were congratulating ourselves on being highly complimented.

At the appointed time, Lieut. Col. Moulton and Capt. Rawlston of somebody's staff put in an appearance. The captain was the inspecting officer; a very airy, pompous young gentleman, with a remarkable faculty of making his weak points conspicuous. When the companies fell in, he noticed the artillery detail did not fall in and inquired the reason. Col. Moulton replied that they were expecting to be inspected as artillery. The captain said he knew nothing about that, he was sent here to inspect this detachment as infantry and every man must fall in. Now that was all right enough, only it placed me at a disadvantage, for I had taken no thought or care of Spitfire since my promotion and it was looking pretty bad. But I had no time to clean it up, and I must say it was a sorry looking piece to take out for a show. But as bad as it looked, I had the utmost confidence in its shooting qualities, in fact I have never lost confidence in Spitfire but once, that was when I dropped it in the creek at Goldsboro.

We were marched out and paraded, and after the inspecting officer had "sassed" Col. Moulton and nearly all the other officers, he commenced his job. He found right smart of fault, but didn't find a really good subject until he came to me. He looked me over, and taking Spitfire gave it a very careful and thorough inspection. Handing it back he very gravely informed me that he had inspected the whole army of the Potomac and had never before seen a rifle looking so bad as Spitfire, and still further complimenting me by saying I was about the roughest looking sergeant he had ever seen. I nodded assent, venturing the remark that I had been in the artillery detail while here and my rifle had been somewhat neglected, but I had a gun on the Malakoff that could knock the spots off the sun. He allowed that that was insolence and any more of it would subject me to arrest. Imagine the indignation of the chief of artillery on being threatened with arrest by an infantry captain. My first impulse was to call my command, lash him to the muzzle of the gun on the Malakoff and give him rapid transit over the tops of the pines, but better thoughts soon succeeded and I forgave him, thinking that perhaps he was doing as well as he knew how. The inspection over, he had not long to stay, as the boat was waiting for him. I noticed the officers didn't pet him very much and I don't believe he got more than one drink.

MISS CARROLL.

Three or four miles out here, through the woods, lives a Mr. Carroll. He has two sons in the 1st North Carolina union volunteers, stationed up in Washington. He makes frequent visits up there to see the boys and is often accompanied by his daughter, a rather good-looking young lady of about 20 years of age. It sometimes happens that they get here early in the morning and have to wait an hour or so for the boat, and will sometimes stop an hour on their return before going home. At these times they are guests at headquarters and a few of us, without the fear of the captain before our eyes, will happen in to have a chat with the old gentleman and his daughter. She expressed a great fondness for literature and claims to be "the only really literary young lady in these yere parts." We occasionally fit her out with such story papers and magazines as we may have lying around, for which she expresses great pleasure.

She one day inquired if we had read a certain piece of poetry in one of the magazines we had given her. She was told we had and thought it very nice. We inquired if she was pleased with it. She replied she thought it was "Splendid! beautiful!" We asked if she was fond of poetry. She said, she was excessively fond of it and read a great deal; in a sly, blushing kind of way, she hinted that she sometimes tried her hand at composing. "Ah, indeed; would you favor us with a few specimens, some day when you come over? We should be pleased to look at them." She promised she would, and the next time she came she brought a composition entitled "Lines to the Union Boys." They were the merest doggerel, but we were loud in their praise and told her that by reading poetry and practising composing she would excel; that when the cruel war was over and we had retired to the peaceful pursuits of life in our far northern homes, we hoped to be reminded of her occasionally, by seeing some of her productions in print. She seemed a good deal pleased with such flattering encomiums, but thought she would hardly attain to that distinction. I thought so too. I asked if she would allow me to take a copy of the lines during her absence up town, and she kindly consented. Below is the copy:

    I suppose you have herd of Swift creek
    An the victory there was won
    The yankee boys was wide awake
    An they made them rebels run.

CHORUS—Farewell Father an Mother
    An a true sweetheart
    An the girls we leave in pain
    Oh dont forget those yankee bys they are coming back again.

    An when the yankees did come in
    The guerrillas took to flight
    An tore down the bonna blue flag
    An hoisted the stars an stripes.

    When South Carolina did secede
    An surely did go out
    The yankee boys must have bin asleep
    They had not whipt her back

    I take my stand in Richmond
    An Swift creek II persue
    I do not care for Whitford*
    Nor none of his cowardly crew

    The gurrillas hates the Buffalows†
    But they dont care for that
    If they dont shut their mouths an let them alone
    They will make them clere the track

    There is good many men in this war
    By the names of Hill
    An if the yankees dus get them
    They will larn them how to drill

*Whitford was a Guerrilla captain.
†Buffaloes were North Carolina Union volunteers.

There is good many men here
By the name of Whitford two
An when the yankees does get them
They will put them rebels through

The secesh girls look mighty loansum
Walking the road in there homemade homespun
The Union girls dont look sad
Walking the road in there yankee plad

An when the war is ended
The guerrillas they will say
They rather fight the devil
Than the boys that gains the day

Hold your toungs you secesh ones
An see what will be don
The yankees boys are bound to go
The whole hog or none

The Union men looks mighty grand
With there cork heel boots an their gloves on their hands
The secesh men looks mighty mean
Going through the woods an never are seen. CHORUS, &c.

Now whatever fault can be found with the above lines, there can certainly no fault be found with their loyalty.

WAITING TO BE RELIEVED.

We keep a small camp guard during the night and this duty is assigned to the artillery detail, each gun's company taking its turn, which brings us on every third night. There are only four posts, the guns and magazine, and as they only go on at tattoo and come off at reveille, the duty is not very arduous. The guard is divided into two reliefs, one going on the first part of the night and the other the latter part; the duty is simply to keep their ears open for any disturbance among the pickets out in the woods and alarm the camp. The reliefs sleep in their quarters and are called when wanted. The sergeant or corporal on duty occupies a small wall tent, in which a candle is kept burning through the night. Having my choice of time and it not making any difference to the corporal, I take the latter part, as I prefer sleeping the first part. I have a splendid corporal, I think the best in the service; we go along together, and agree first rate. He is willing to do all the work and I am willing he should. He posts the first relief and then keeps his eyes open until it is time to post the second relief, when he posts them and then comes and calls me, when I relieve him. My work is now all done; all I have to do is to lie down and go to sleep or busy myself with my reading or writing, and call off the relief at reveille. If I am too busy to attend to that duty (which I generally am), they take the responsibility of relieving themselves, which is a great help to me and relieves me of a great burden of care.

One night while on this duty the officer of the day came in

and inquired if I would like to take a stroll and make a round of the pickets. I replied that I should. We started out making the round and not being in a hurry did not get back till daylight. I laid down and went to sleep, feeling that everything was all safe and quiet on the Pamlico. About 7 o'clock I was called up and told I was wanted at the magazine. I went out and there stood Charley, a Roman sentinel amid the wreck of worlds. I admired his fidelity, but I really couldn't commend his judgment and no explanation or excuses of mine availed in the least; he was going to be relieved officially, and after he had got through with me I don't think there were many more cuss words left in him. I certainly felt relieved if he didn't.

THE ROVER.

Capt. Foss somewhere picked up an old boat and with Jed's assistance put it in good repair, rigged up a sail, rated it A 1, and named it the Rover. The captain is skipper and Jed sailing master. She is a long, clipper-built craft, with a large spread of canvas and a carrying capacity of ten or twelve persons. With a spanking breeze she walks up and down the river like a thing of life and makes nothing of sailing right around the little steamer Undine. She makes frequent trips to Rodman's and occasionally to town. The captain selects the party he wants to take out and I am sometimes honored with an invitation. We usually run alongside the gunboat that lays here and take aboard the second assistant engineer, who is a genial, good-natured old fellow, full of his fun and stories, and then put for Rodman's. We stop there an hour and start for home. On the return trip, the old engineer's inventive powers will be a good deal quickened and he will suggest various alterations in the rig and sail of the craft, which will improve her sailing qualities, all of which Jed readily accepts and is going to forthwith adopt, but the next day the improvements are all forgotten and never thought of again until another return trip from Rodman's. A few days ago a small party of us made a halt at Rodman's and found Sergeant Martin in command. He did the honors, showing us about the camp and extending hospitalities in a manner that would have done credit to a prince. To my notion Sergeant Martin has got the correct idea of holding a command, not to go dry himself nor let his friends.

BIG JIM.

Big Jim, as he is called, is a character; genial, charitable, good-natured, humorous and generous to a fault. He is quite a theatrical character and loves to deal in romance and tragedy, and he caters to the mirthful and fun-loving among the boys. He does not amount to much as a soldier, but that is more his misfortune than from any unwillingness. He is of enormous proportions and very fat, tipping the scale at 250 pounds. He is sorely troubled with chafing when drilling or on the march, and for that reason is excused from pretty much all duty. He is a sort of independent corps, doing duty when he feels like it; he will often go out in the woods and relieve a man on picket who happens to be taken sick. He sometimes has a feeling come over him that he would like to get away from the noise and bustle of the camp, and be alone by himself. At such times he takes his rifle and goes to the little point, some 100 rods down the river, where there is a picket post. Here he will stay two or three days at a time, caring for no company except at night, and amuses himself with fishing, reading and writing. He has become so enamoured of this kind of life, that he has taken the contract to do the picket duty at that post and has made it his permanent residence, coming up to camp only two or three times a week to see the boys and get his rations. He has opened a trading post down there, and trades with the natives who touch there as they come in their boats from up the bay or cove which sets back from there. He has built himself a log house, and a sign over the door reads "Cash paid for coon skins," of which and other peltries he has collected quite a quantity, and intends sending them to Boston markets.

FURLOUGH.

SEPT. 20. Our last furloughed men have returned, and I have the promise of one next week, and am congratulating myself on the prospect of once more seeing home. I am anticipating a great deal when I get home; among other things the pleasure of once more sitting down to a clean, well-spread table, with a good square dinner before me. In anticipation of such an event, I send by this mail a small bill of fare of such dishes as I think I shall relish, and have ordered them to be ready and smoking hot on my arrival:

Roast—Sirloin of beef, spare rib of pork, breast of veal, turkey with cranberry sauce, chicken.

Baked—Bluefish, oyster dressing. Chicken pie.

Boiled—Halibut. Fried—Ponts.

Chicken salad. Lobster salad.

Oysters—Stewed, fried, escalloped. Clam chowder.

27 dozen Providence river oysters on the half shell.

Mashed potatoes, boiled onions, beets, turnips, squash, sweet corn, string beans, succotash, stewed tomatoes, tomatoes sliced with vinegar or sugar, apple dumplings with sugar sauce; mince, apple, berry, lemon, cream and custard pie.

Also one moderately sized pumpkin pie, say about thirty-six inches across and not less than eight inches deep; that is as small a pumpkin pie as I care to bother with.

Oranges, apples, pears, grapes, chestnuts, walnuts, cider.

N. B. No boiled salt pork, beef soup or rice and molasses. I don't hanker for that.

With that bill of fare, and such other things as my folks will naturally think of, I reckon I can make a tolerable dinner.

CHAPTER VI.

NEWPORT NEWS, VA., DEC. 1, 1863. On receipt of my furlough, which came promptly to hand at the appointed time, I, in company with eight others from the three companies, left Hill's Point for Massachusetts. I had 25 days at home, a part of which I used up on the lounge, with chills and fever, and listening to the expressions of sympathy from callers. Ordinarily, when a person is sick, it is pleasant to be surrounded by sympathizing friends, but a person with chills and fever does not want sympathy; that only makes him mad. What he wants is whiskey and quinine, and the more whiskey the better. I was asked if the disease ever terminated fatally. I replied that the most provoking thing about it was, there was not the slightest danger of dying from it. After recovering from the chills and fever, I enjoyed the balance of my visit very much, and reported back in New York the next morning after the expiration of my furlough.

Arriving in New York, I went directly to the New England rooms on Broadway. These rooms are a kind of free hotel for New England soldiers en route through New York, but will accommodate any others when they are not full. The rooms are well fitted up and there is a spacious loft or hall which is used for sleeping with 100 or more single cots, on each of which is a good mattress, pillow, a pair of woolen blankets and white spread. In this room a man is in attendance day and night to attend to the wants of patrons, preserve order and look after things generally. The dining hall will seat about 200 persons, and the tables are well supplied with plain, substantial, wholesome food. Another room is used for a sick room or hospital, and is filled up with a few cots and lounges, and the tables are well supplied with books and newspapers. This room is presided over by a kind-hearted, sympathetic lady, who was formerly a hospital matron in McClellan's peninsular campaign. Besides, there is the office and baggage room, where one's knapsack or other baggage is put away and checked. The owner takes his check and gives no further thought or care of his baggage until wanted. In addition to these, are all other necessary conveniences. These rooms were fitted up and are supported by the patriotic generosity of New Englanders, residents in New York, and many are the thanks and blessings they receive from their beneficiaries. Here I found Spencer and Lewis, who were furloughed with me, and who had just arrived. The clerk told us we must report to a certain quartermaster up town for instructions. We reported: he examined our papers, endorsed on the backs "reported back all right and on time," and told us we must report at the transportation office down near the battery park. We reported, and were informed there was no transportation waiting, but we must report every morning in order to avail ourselves of the first boat that left.

RECLINING ON OUR MILITARY.

There were 100 or more soldiers waiting transportation to Newbern, besides hundreds of others for all parts of the army. The officer in charge of the office would no more than get his coat off and sleeves rolled up, ready for business in the morning, when we would appear to him. He would get rid of us by a wave of his hand and "No boat for Newbern." This continued for several mornings, until he became tired of seeing us and hung a card on the door with "No boat for Newbern."

One morning the card was off and all hands made a grand charge inside. He gave us the cheering information that Gen. Foster had moved his old brigade from Newbern to Fortress Monroe, and he would give transportation by way of Baltimore to as many of us as belonged to that brigade. No one seemed to know just what to do, and no reply was made to the statement. After waiting a few moments, he inquired what we were going to do. As no one spoke, I ventured the remark that I had received no official information of the removal of the brigade or of my regiment and until further orders, I thought I had better stick to the order in my furlough and report in North Carolina. That seemed to clear away the cloud that hung over the boys, and we were soon on the street again.

The next morning, however, the clouds thickened again. The officer said he had reliable information that the 23d, 25th and 27th Massachusetts and 9th New Jersey regiments, together with the 3d New York cavalry, were at Fortress Monroe; he was going to give orders for rations and transportation by way of Baltimore to all those belonging to those regiments, and we could come in the afternoon and get them. I inquired if he was authorized to order us to report at Fortress Monroe. That gave him a sort of blind staggers. He said he was not really, but it would be all right enough, especially if we were anxious to join our regiments.

I replied, "We are anxious to join our regiments, but as everything in military has to run in its regular groove, and as one order holds good until another is given, it would hardly look military to be acting on our own judgment and hearsay stories, and going off across lots, reporting somewhere else than where our orders say."

"You seem to be right on your military. Do you always pay as strict observance to orders?"

"That is the way we have been educated, sir."

That question settled, we were soon on the pave again.

AN ENCOUNTER WITH A POLICEMAN.

During our long wait for transportation we had a fine chance of doing the city, an opportunity of which we availed ourselves in the most thorough manner. We visited all places of interest and everywhere that there was anything to be seen or heard. One day Spencer and I, after a long ramble over the city, wandered into City Hall park, and feeling rather tired sat down on the City Hall steps to rest and watch the passing throng. We had not sat there many minutes when a policeman came along, and pointing to us with his cane, said: "You can't sit there," and passed along. We regarded that as a sort of camp rumor and kept our sitting. He presently returned, and coming up to us in a very imperious manner, said: "How many times do you fellows want to be told that you can't sit there?" I looked at him, and with all the innocence and simplicity I could assume, I said: "You see, sir, that we *do* sit here." That shot struck below the water line, and he then said: "What I mean is, you are not allowed to sit there." "Ah! in that case we will remove hence, as you will observe by our raiment that we are preservers, rather than breakers, of law."

A VISIT TO BARNUM'S.

The outside of Barnum's Museum is always covered with immense show bills and people have become so accustomed to them that they attract but little attention, unless it is some new and curious thing he has got on exhibition. Noticing a picture of an enormous sea lion and reading glowing descriptions of him in the newspapers, I remarked to Spencer: "We had better take that in." Now Barnum's is a good place to go, as it is a highly moral show, and inexpensive—twenty-five cents giving one the whole range from basement to attic. Taking those things into consideration he thought we had better go, so one evening we went up.

Exchanging our quarters at the office for tickets we were admitted to the great show. After strolling around awhile and looking at some of the minor curiosities, we went down into the basement where is located the aquarium. We soon found the sea lion. He laid on a large platform with his head towards the grating and about three feet from it. At the rear end of the platform was a large tank of water where he could bathe. He was a harmless looking lion enough and resembled a mule as much as a lion. He looked like pictures I have seen of the walrus, and laid there, a huge jelly-looking mass apparently dead, but on close inspection respiration was observable. We tried to start him up, but he seemed to prefer quiet, and no motion with our arms and caps had the slightest effect on him. I had an uncontrollable desire to see him go into the tank, and looked in vain all around the place for something to stir him up with. Presently a gentleman came along and stopped to look at him. He had an umbrella and I asked him to stir the creature up and see him go into the water. But he thought he had better not, saying it was probably against the rules for visitors to disturb him. I said that was probably the case, but we had paid our money to come into the show and wanted to see all the tricks, and if he would let me take the umbrella I would stir him up and take the responsibility. But he declined, and moved on.

A bright thought now struck me; I would fill his eye with tobacco juice and see what effect that would have. I chewed up a large piece of tobacco; filling my mouth with the juice and getting a beautiful range on his left eye, let drive, covering it completely, and to my utter astonishment that creature never so much as winked. I was dumbfounded at the result of my experiment, as this was the first creature I had ever seen which had eyes that a little tobacco juice in them would not make things lively for a few minutes. I can account for my failure in no other way than that, being a marine animal, there is probably some kind of film or covering over the eye that protects it from foreign substances while in the water. Spencer laughed at my discomfiture, and said perhaps we could find something else I would have better luck experimenting with.

Strolling around up stairs we came to the mummy cabinet. Now I like mummies and am always interested in them; they have a habit of minding their own business the steadiest of any class of people I ever met with, besides they are always civil to callers and are free from the disputes, quarrels, gossipping, slanders and other vices with which our generation is afflicted. They are a very ancient people, and in their time were doubtless an intelligent and highly respectable class of citizens, but they don't amount to much now; they are too far behind the times and I don't think it would be of much use for them to try to catch up. In this cabinet was quite a large collection and they looked black and dirty as though they neglected their baths and toilets; they all looked so much alike it was difficult to distinguish their sex. I think if they could be taken out and washed and dressed up in fashionable clothing they would make quite a respectable appearance.

I looked around to find some biographies of these people but could not. I called the attention of an attendant and inquired of him if there was any. He replied there was none that he knew of. I then asked: "Is Mr. Barnum about the place? I should like to see him." He stated that Mr. Barnum was away and inquired my business with him. I said I wanted to suggest to Mr. Barnum that if he would hang a biography on every one of these mummies it would be the most taking thing he ever had, not excepting the What-is-it. This attendant somehow didn't seem to get interested in Barnum's interests, and dodged off out of the way. I pointed out the largest one to Spencer and said: "That gentleman was once a soldier and did provost duty in the city of Thebes 3000 years ago." He made no reply but kept looking at it and presently I heard him muttering to himself: "Can that be possible? Brave old fossil!"

We got up into the exhibition room, near the close of the play; they were playing the ghost. I should think it might be a good enough play, but the acting was not all that a connoisseur would accept, but then it was good enough for soldiers and the price. I thought the ghost illusion was very cleverly performed, but Spencer said it was tame compared with the Gum swamp trick.

OFF FOR NEWBERN.

After waiting thirteen days a boat arrived and we were now off. The boat leaves in the afternoon and all hands go down to the transportation office to get our orders and say good bye to the genial officer in command. I noticed that my draft for rations was on the Park barracks. Now I had a dim recollection and a sort of instinctive horror of those barracks, and it occurred to me that I had seen down on the Battery park, near the water, a small building where was kept first class rations, which were dealt out to officers, and other attaches of the army as department and sutler's clerks and such like nobility. I suggested to Spencer that we go down there; we could fix up some kind of a story and perhaps succeed in getting our rations.

Now Spencer is a conscientious young man and objects to anything that does not dovetail in the exact line of right and honor. He objected to going, saying we should have to tell some extravagant stories and then get nothing, and perhaps get ourselves into some trouble. I said we would make only a plain statement of facts; that we are living in perilous times and that the end would justify the means.

We went down there and the only regalia the supervisor of the place had on that denoted any rank in the army was a pair of blue pants; just what rank he held we were unable to determine by those pants. We showed him our orders. He looked at them and said: "What are you here for? Go up to the Park barracks where your orders say."

"Yes, I know; but we have just come from there; they are all full up there and are running short of rations; they sent us down here."

"Don't believe a word of it; they have no business to be short of rations up there and have no business to send you here anyway, and I don't believe they did."

"You, sir, have a perfect right to *believe* just what you please, but here is an order for rations; the boat leaves in about an hour and if we don't have the rations we shall not go in her, and if we don't go it will be somebody's fault."

Thinking perhaps that tracing out faults might prove unpleasant, he pointed us to a tub of boiled corned beef and a basket of soft bread, telling us to take as little as would do us. To allay any fears he might have on that score, we said we did not care to burden ourselves with any superfluous freight. We not only took the meat and bread he told us to, but helped ourselves liberally to some boiled ham and raw onions that stood near by against his most emphatic protest. So, with some lying on our part and considerable swearing on his part, we succeeded in supplying ourselves with first-class rations.

When we came out, Spencer said: "I was shocked to hear you lie so."

"But I have not been lying."

"Well, then, I should like to know what you would call it?"

"What I said might possibly be twisted and contorted into something that would give it the appearance of lying, but I have only made a few positive statements, and as I said before the end justifies the means."

That statement seemed to satisfy him, and a little while after we were aboard the steamer Albany, bound for Newbern. Standing on the quarter-deck as we steamed down the harbor and through the narrows,

> We watched the big city with curious eye,
> 'Till the last towering dome had gone out in the sky.

We arrived at Newbern after a four days' passage and reported to the provost marshal, Capt. Denny of our regiment, who welcomed us back and gave us the liberty of the city. He informed us the regiment was at Fortress Monroe, and if we had only known it while in New York, we could have saved ourselves the trouble of coming here and having to go back. We were somewhat surprised at this intelligence, and disappointed at not knowing it while there, and saving ourselves all this unnecessary trouble and delay. But, however, we must put up with it, and take the next boat back which leaves for Fortress Monroe.

After a four days' visit here we went aboard the little steamer Vidette, bound for Fortress Monroe. We had aboard about 200 soldiers and about 100 Confederate prisoners. We left in the afternoon and the next morning were at Hatteras inlet. The sea was pretty rough, and in crossing the swash we fouled with a schooner, carrying away her bowsprit and losing one of our anchors. The old captain, who by the way was a jolly old fellow, said he never had so good luck before in getting through the inlet; he had only lost an anchor and taken off a schooner's bowsprit. As we went past the battery, he yelled out to them to fish up his anchor against he got back.

The following morning we were at Fortress Monroe and here learned that our regiment was at Newport News, at the mouth of the James river. We re-shipped on another boat, and an hour after were receiving the ovations and congratulations of our comrades, after an absence of nearly two months.

NEWPORT NEWS.

DEC. 10. I am now on the sacred soil of old Virginia, and my first care will be to seek an introduction to some of the F. F. V's. What this place derived its name from, or why it was named at all, I have not been able to learn. It was simply a plantation before its occupation by Federal troops, and perhaps the name is as good as any to distinguish it by. Our camp is near the river, and only a few rods from us lie the wrecks of the frigates Cumberland and Congress, sunk by the rebel ram Merrimac. The Cumberland lies in deep water out of sight, but the deck of the Congress is seen and often visited by the boys at low water. Since the occupation of this place by Federal troops it has grown into what they call down this way a town, containing quite a collection of rough board store-houses, sutler's shops, negro shanties and horse sheds. A boat runs from here to Fortress Monroe every day, and three times a week to Norfolk; the distance to either place is about the same, some twelve miles.

For the first time since the war began, the oyster fishing is being prosecuted, and Hampton Roads are alive with oyster schooners. The oysters have had a chance to grow, and are now abundant and of good size and flavor. Newport News was the first place in Virginia, except Washington, that was occupied by Federal troops, and it was from here that a part of old Ben's famous Big Bethel expedition started.

During my absence, this military department has gone all wrong. Gen. Foster has been ordered to Knoxville, Tenn., and Gen. Butler has superseded him to this command. I am not pleased with the change. Gen. Foster was a splendid man and fine officer, and I would rather take my chances with a regular army officer than with an amateur. The first year of the war Gen. Butler was the busiest and most successful general we had, but since then he has kind o' taken to niggers and trading. As a military governor he is a nonesuch, and in that role has gained a great fame, especially in all the rebellious states. He is a lawyer and a man of great executive ability, and can not only make laws but can see to it that they are observed, but as a commander of troops in the field, he is not just such a man as I should pick out. He had a review of our brigade the other day, and his style of soldiering caused considerable fun among the boys who had been used to seeing Gen. Foster. He rode on to the field with a great dash, followed by staff enough for two major-generals. He looks very awkward on a horse and wears a soft hat; when he salutes the colors he lifts his hat by the crown clear off his head instead of simply touching the rim. The boys think he is hardly up to their ideas of a general, but as they are not supposed to know anything, they will have to admit that he *is* a great general. He is full of orders and laws (regardless of army regulations) in the government of his department, and his recent order in relation to darkies fills two columns of newspaper print, and is all the most fastidious lovers of darkies in all New England could desire. Hunter and Fremont are the merest pigmies beside Ben in their care of darkies.

RE-ENLISTING.

JANUARY 1, 1864. We have now entered on the last year of our soldier service and are looking forward to the end, and may it not only end our service as soldiers, but the war as well, when both sides can meet between the lines, shake hands, smoke the pipe of peace and together sign a long and lasting truce, and all say homeward bound. But I am sermonising, and however much that happy end may be desired, the indications now are that it will not be realized. For a month past our regiment has been a good deal excited. About thirty days ago orders were received from the war department at Washington, soliciting re-enlistments from among the soldiers of the old regiments of 1861. Liberal money inducements were offered, and in addition the present term of service would end on re-enlistment; the $100 bounty due at the expiration of the three years term could be drawn, together with a thirty day's furlough. Lieut. Woodworth of company H was appointed recruiting officer, but up to the present time there have been but few enlistments. We all understood the terms and all thus far have been left free to act according to their own judgment. The officers have not seemed to take much interest in it and have not used their influence to get the boys to enlist but have given advice when sought for. If a man re-enlists he has some motive for it; if he does not he has his reasons, and both may be equally patriotic. I shall not re-enlist, and my reasons are, first, I have no desire to monopolize all the patriotism there is, but am willing to give others a chance. My second reason is that after I have served three years my duty to the country has been performed and my next duty is at home with my family.

JAN. 14. Up to this date about 200 of our men have re-enlisted, and today the first detachment left for home on their thirty days' furlough. They were accompanied by three of the officers, one of whom was Lieut. McCarter of company B. I hope they will have a good time and enjoy themselves. Orders keep coming from headquarters at the fort to hurry up enlistments and some of them are of a rather threatening character.

JAN. 17. The balance of the re-enlisted men left for home today, several of the officers going with them. We have now got our ultimatum, either enlist or go into exile. An order was received intimating that as enlistments seemed about through in this regiment, we would be more useful at Yorktown than here, and for us to be ready to march in heavy marching order at any time; but enlistments still drag.

JAN. 18. The order has arrived and we are under heavy marching orders for Yorktown, which is 30 miles distant and where, it is said, we shall probably all die of malarial fever or other contagious diseases. But there is one redeeming feature to the order; that is, if we will enlist, or three-fourths of those reported for duty will enlist, then they can all go home together as a regiment, while those not enlisting will be sent into banishment, the non-coms reduced to the ranks and permanently assigned to other organizations during their terms of enlistment.

JAN. 20. Yesterday and today have been busy days at Camp Upton. The idea of going home as a regiment has found favor with the officers, and as this is the last day of grace they have been raising heaven and earth to get us to enlist. They have had us out on the parade ground using all their powers of persuasion and eloquence for enlistments, and have succeeded in enlisting nearly the whole regiment. I have reported these speeches and when I get them fixed up with all the necessary embellishments and illustrations, they will make an interesting chapter of literature.

JAN. 21. It now appears there are 225 of us who go into exile. We are to take all our earthly effects with us and get them along as best we can, notwithstanding a boat goes around with our camp equipage and might just as well take us, but that would be no punishment for our stubbornness. In justice to our officers, however, I learn that they endeavored to get transportation for our knapsacks but were not successful. We took our last dinner with the boys at Camp Upton, and at 2 p. m. were in line awaiting marching orders. Capt. Parkhurst is in command; Lieuts. Johnson and Saul, with Assistant Surgeon Hoyt accompany us. As we stand waiting orders the officers and boys gather around us and a feeling of sadness seems to pervade the whole crowd at the thought that this is the dissolution of the old regiment. Mutual handshakings and best wishes are exchanged, we say good-bye and move off.

                And so they parted,
    The angel up to heaven and Adam to his bower.

THE FAMOUS MARCH OF THE FAMOUS TWO HUNDRED.

WILLIAMSBURG, VA., JAN. 25. Leaving Newport News on the afternoon of the 21st, we made a march of about ten miles, reaching Little Bethel just before dark, when we halted and put up in an old church building for the night. Little Bethel contains beside the church an old grist and saw mill, a blacksmith shop and three small houses, all in a rather dilapidated condition. There was no enemy within 100 miles of us, but Capt. Parkhurst, either as a matter of form or through force of habit, put out a few pickets. The old church had long ago been stripped of its seats and pulpit, if it ever had any, leaving the whole floor unobstructed. After supper and getting a little rested, a dance was proposed. A gallery extended across one end, and on the front of this the candles were thickly set, lighting up the old church in fine style. One of our German comrades of Company G had a violin and furnished the music. Sets were formed and the fun commenced. The pickets outside, hearing the sounds of revelry within, left their posts and came in, and standing their rifles in a corner threw off their equipments and joined in the dance. The captain remonstrated at such unlawful proceedings, but the cry was "Never mind the pickets! on with the dance! let fun be unrestrained." The dance was kept up until the candles burned low, when we spread our blankets and laid down for rest.

In the morning we found outside five men with their horses and carts, waiting to sell us oysters. Fortunately we were the possessors of a few scraps of paper bearing the signature of Uncle Samuel. With a portion of this paper we bought the men's oysters, and after breakfast we chartered them to carry our knapsacks to Yorktown, thereby nullifying the order of the great Mogul at Fortress Monroe, and I have not the slightest doubt that if he knew of it he would hang every one of those men for giving aid and comfort to the incorrigible.

Leaving Little Bethel we marched over McClellan's famous corduroy road through white oak swamp, coming out at Warwick court house. This is a county seat, containing a small court house situated in a pretty grove of trees, a jail, church, half a dozen houses and a blacksmith shop. We arrived at the forks of the roads, a mile below and in full view of historic old Yorktown, about the middle of the afternoon. Here we were met by an officer and commanded to halt till further orders. I thought this was as near as they dared have us come the first day for fear the malaria would strike us too suddenly.

From here the dim outlines of Washington's old intrenchments could be traced and near by was what appeared to be an angle in the line on which guns were probably mounted and which commanded the whole open plain between here and town. Now it did not require a great stretch of the imagination to go back to those days and see those brave men toiling and suffering behind those works, to build up for themselves and their posterity a country and a name. I could see in my mind the haughty Cornwallis march out upon this plain, surrendering his army and his sword to Washington, in the last grand act in the drama of the American revolution. But how is it today? Yonder rebel fort tells in thunder tones how well their degenerate sons appreciate the legacy.

About dusk an orderly rode up, bringing an order for us to proceed to Williamsburg, some fifteen miles further up the country. We tried to get the captain to stop here till morning and go through the next day, but it was of no use; he had got his orders to march and was going through tonight. I could not see that it was a military necessity to force the march, and after we had gone three or four miles my knapsack began to grow heavy and I grew tired. I halted by the roadside and said I was going to put up for the night and if any one would like to keep me company I should be pleased to have them. About twenty rallied to my standard. After the column had passed we stepped through a low hedge of bushes into a small open space, surrounded by high bushes which served as a shelter from the winds. Here we spread our blankets and laid ourselves down to forget in our slumbers the weight of our knapsacks. The stars looked down on us and the watchful eye of the Almighty was the only sentinel.

When we awoke in the morning the rising sun's bright ray was peeping through the bushes. The first object which met our gaze was a lean, lank, sandy-complexioned, long-haired native, who stood peering over the bushes at us. The first salutation that greeted his ears was, "Who are you and what do you want?" He replied, "I seed you was down yere, and thought I would come down and see if I could get some 'baccer?" Looking up we saw a house out in the field some distance off, and asked him if he resided there. He said he did. We gave him some tobacco and inquired about the roads and distance to Williamsburg. We inquired if there were any bushwhackers about here? He said "There mought be once in a while one found." Then we put on a ferocious look and said they had better not be found by us unless they wished to join the antediluvian society and have their bones scattered in every graveyard from here to Jerusalem. The old chap's eyes stuck out and he began to edge off, thinking perhaps we had got on a thick coat of war paint. We made our coffee and started on our journey, and by easy stages came up with the boys in the afternoon. They had pitched the camp and got it all fixed up and named Camp Hancock.

I thought the captain was as glad to see us as anyone, but he put on a stern look and inquired where we had been and why we fell out. We told him we were tired and lay down by the side of the road to rest and take a nap. He lectured us on the enormity of such proceedings, telling us we had committed a very flagrant breach of good order and military *despotism*. We assented to all the captain said, but kept thinking all the time that as we were a sort of outcasts, did not belong anywhere and were under no particular command, there wouldn't much come of it.

VISITORS.

JAN. 27. We had been here only two days when our common sense and judgment were still further imposed upon by three of our former officers from the News, soliciting enlistments. They probably thought that a fifty mile march and being in a strange city had perhaps taken the stiffening out of us somewhat, but they were not long in finding out that that was a delusion. Capt. Parkhurst laughed at them, telling them they had come to the wrong market to peddle their wares; the boys crowded around them, giving them scarcely breathing room, and jokingly told them they had picked some chickens the night before, but had got no tar, but perhaps molasses would answer for a substitute. Finding they had come on a fool's errand, they then wanted Surgeon Hoyt to put as many of us on the sick list as possible, thereby increasing the working force at the News. The surgeon told them that men who could make a fifty mile march, carrying heavy knapsacks, were not supposed to be very seriously indisposed. Finding the leopard hadn't changed his spots, they left, taking with them *two* captives.

A CHANGE OF COMMANDERS.

JAN. 29. Today we were paraded and invited to give our attention to orders. Major Mulcay of the 139th New York volunteers appeared on the ground, and read his orders relieving Capt. Parkhurst of the command. He then assumed command, and had a short drill and dress parade. Of course we put the best side out, to give the major a favorable impression. He complimented us for our good drill and neat appearance. Orders were read for a long and rapid march; of course that is one of our kind and we are expected to go on it. The major tells us we shall stay here a few days and then be assigned to his regiment.

SPECULATIONS.

FEB. 1. Since being here we have had but little else to do than make up our diaries, write letters and talk over the situation. The last link is broken that bound us to our old regiment. Capt. Parkhurst, Lieuts. Johnson and Saul and Doctor Hoyt left us yesterday, and we are now thinking of applying for admission to the orphans' home. The boys are all at sea, without chart or compass, and can form no idea of what kind of a landing they will make. The non-coms, of whom there are quite a number, are a good deal exercised over their fate, and are consulting together much of the time. I tell them there is no use trying to lift the veil, but to take things as they come and trust to luck. We can look forward to the end, which is only a few months hence, and during that time we shall probably not be very much worse off than we have been, and certainly can be no worse off than the crowd we are in.

In a talk with Corporal Whipple and a few others, I said I had no fears of our losing our rank, that is if Gen. Sherman is good military authority, which I think he is. Sometime last summer there was some talk at the war department at Washington in regard to consolidating the old regiments. In a letter from Gen. Sherman to the adjutant-general, he said it would be the worst thing for the army that could be done, for in consolidating the old regiments, they would lose a large number of well-trained and efficient soldiers whose places could not easily be filled. For instance, two regiments are consolidated in one, all the officers from colonel to corporal in one of them are lost. They would have to be mustered out and sent home, thereby losing upwards of 150 well-trained men; and he advised instead of consolidating or forming new organizations, to recruit the old ones to their full strength. Now if what he said is law, then when two organizations are consolidated, or one of them is permanently assigned to the other, then one of them loses its officers. Therefore, if we are permanently assigned to some other regiment, and are not wanted as non-commissioned officers, then they can muster us out and send us home.

We have dress parades every night and keep hearing something about the coming march. Whatever it is or wherever we are going, it is getting pretty well advertised. Every night at dress parade, orderlies are seen flying about from camp to camp, carrying their orders, and citizens are standing around with their mouths and ears open catching every word, and if they have any communications with the outside world (which they probably have), then this expedition, whatever it is, will not amount to much. If this thing is being managed by Gen. Butler, which from the pomp and circumstance attending it certainly looks a good deal like him, then in my opinion, it will be another Big Bethel affair.

CAMP WEST.

FEB. 5. Yesterday afternoon Camp Hancock became a thing of the past. Under command of Major Mulcay, we marched on to the parade ground of the 139th New York during their dress parade, and before it was dismissed, the major marched us up and introduced us to Col. Roberts. The colonel received us cordially, and complimented us for our soldierly bearing and the good appearance of our arms, equipments and uniforms. We then listened to the reading of an order, assigning us temporarily for duty to this command. A gleam of light now dawned on us. Col. Roberts again addressed us, saying we were here only during the absence of our own regiment, and would hold the same rank and perform the same duties we had done in our own regiment. He added: "Although among strangers, with not a single officer of your own, I know by your appearance and from what I have heard of you, that you will as willingly observe your orders and perform your duties as cheerfully as you have done heretofore." Then addressing his own regiment, he said: "Receive these men cordially, sharing with them your quarters and blankets, and in all ways treating them as you would like to be treated under similar circumstances." We made the welkin ring with cheers for Col. Roberts and his command, which were responded to by the 139th. After this another order was read, stating that the long expected march would commence tomorrow morning, the 6th. Col. Roberts, after addressing a few remarks to his own regiment, turned to us and said: "To you of the 25th Massachusetts, I have nothing to say. You know your duty and I am satisfied you will perform it."

We were then divided off into parties which would equalize the companies of the regiment; the balance, about 25, were sent to Fort Magruder, which is only a short distance away. A dozen others and myself were assigned to company I, Capt. Phillips. The boys were warmly welcomed, and all set about introducing themselves to each other and getting acquainted. This camp is constructed of small log houses, with board floors and glass windows. The houses are furnished with stoves, chairs, stools, table and sleeping bunks. The officers' quarters are built of logs with the bark left on, and are large and roomy. Some of them are two stories, others are neat little cottages built in Gothic style, and all present a neat, attractive and artistic appearance. These houses are all supplied and furnished with home comforts, some of them containing cabinet organs. The officers have with them their wives, sisters and other female relatives, who fancy the romance and rough experience of a soldiers' camp. This is a Brooklyn regiment; it has been out but little more than a year and has been stationed here all this time, so the men have had the opportunity to fix up their camp to suit them. Their first and only service was with Gen. Dix, when he went up the country towards Richmond in the fall of 1862. Since then they have done picket duty around here, and some scouting up in the woods beyond the town.

They seem to have a mortal horror of bushwhackers, and say the woods above here are full of them, with some guerilla bands. It would seem from what these fellows say that the principle business of these guerilla bands is to look out for prisoners escaping from Richmond, and in connection with bushwhackers, to harass small parties of troops who are sent out to look after them. The scouting parties which go out seem to think that the proper way to deal with bushwhackers is to capture them, but scarcely a party goes out without bringing back one or more of their own number either dead or wounded. It is only two days ago I saw a funeral from the camp of the New York First Mounted Rifles of a man who had been killed up there. I tell the

Brooklyn boys that the best use a bushwhacker can be put to is to make a target of him, and be sure to hit the bull's eye when you draw a bead on him; never make a prisoner of one. The Brooklynites are asking our boys a thousand questions, and the latter are telling them blood and thunder stories till the former have come to think we are the veritable heroes of Waterloo.

Our friends here seem to be anxious and troubled about the morrow, wondering what kind of a scrape they are going to get into and whether they will come out all right, and are probing to the bottom the dark side of the matter. I try to cheer them up by telling them that from what experience I have had in this business I am not anticipating much of a storm. It has been too long underway and has been too well advertised; we may have a skirmish, nothing more. If the force around here is all that is going, we shall have to look out and not get into much of a skirmish.

The mystery which has for so many days hung over us is at last cleared up, and Gen. Butler, after finding we were not to be driven nor frightened, has in his order assigning us temporarily for duty, acknowledged he was exceeding his authority in threatening us with permanent assignment and taking our warrants from us. If it had been some other general who didn't know any better I should think he was relenting of his shabby treatment of us, but Gen. Butler *knew* better, and that makes his treatment of us all the more reprehensible. I presume we shall have to get ourselves and knapsacks back to the News the same way we got here, although there are boats running round twice and three times a week.

THE EXPEDITION.

FEB. 11. The morning of February 6th found us in line on the parade ground, New York and Massachusetts shoulder to shoulder. Capt. Phillips, wanting a brave and valiant veteran on the left of his company, assigned me to that post of honor. I reckon the reason for it was that two of his sergeants were on the sick list. While standing in line, waiting the order to march, a scene is transpiring which to us of the 25th is altogether new and strange. The ladies living here in camp are all out, and wetting their handkerchiefs with their tears, are watching the preparations to leave. They are struggling under a fearful burden of anxiety which will not be removed until our return. Groups of men and women are standing around, taking each other by the hand and kissing their good-byes. Our Brooklyn friends are visibly affected, while the 25th boys look on stoically. While men and women with streaming eyes are bidding perhaps their last farewells, these roughened, hardened sons of Mars look with unpitying eye on this affecting scene and laugh. I confess I should have taken a greater interest in the thing and my sympathies would have flowed more freely if I could have taken a hand in the kissing.

We marched into town where the brigade line was formed, consisting of the 139th and 118th New York, two regiments of colored troops and one U. S. battery, (the 2d I think). The mounted rifles were to follow later. This comprised the whole force under command of Brig. Gen. Wistar, whoever he is. The line of march was taken up the country on the road towards Richmond. Arriving at the woods, about a mile from town, the column was halted and a detail made to act as skirmishers. The 139th being on the advance furnished the detail. In this detail the 25th was largely represented, and was under command of Major Mulcay. The major marched his command a few rods into the woods, formed his skirmish line and ordered them forward, the column following. I now began to hear plenty of talk about bushwhackers and business for the boys ahead. Capt. Phillips fell back to the rear of his company, marching by my side. I thought this a good opportunity to scrape an acquaintance, and commenced talking to him, but he did not seem to be in a mood for conversation and said as little as possible. He commenced a low, suppressed whistle of a single strain of Rally 'Round the Flag. I tried all means I could think of to draw him out, but finding I could do nothing with him, I turned my attention to the major and his skirmishers. He was as busy with them and as particular as if they were out for skirmish drill, and kept talking to them all the time about preserving their distances and alignments.

After a time, the boys started up a rabbit, and half a dozen of them gave chase, shouting and yelling till they were out of sight in the woods, where they waited for the major to come up. The major lectured them a little about charging without orders and warning them of the great danger they were in from bushwhackers. All the thanks he got from those heartless fellows for all his care and solicitude was: "Oh! damn the bushwhackers!" and as soon as another rabbit or squirrel was started up, away they would go again. Capt. Phillips, who meanwhile had kept up his whistle, suppressed it long enough to say: "Your boys are taking great risks in running off into the woods in that way; some of them will get shot by bushwhackers." I said I thought our boys had very little fear of bushwhackers, and would sooner have the fun of chasing them than rabbits, besides I thought there was little danger from bushwhackers, for when a force like this was marching through they preferred keeping at a safe distance.

A little after noon the cavalry overtook us, and we halted to let them go past us. I was surprised to see such a force; there was a whole brigade, numbering between 3000 and 4000, under command of Col. Spear, who had been sent down from the army of the Potomac, landing at Yorktown, and had now overtaken us. I could now begin to see through a glass darkly. This is the raid on Richmond, of which I had heard some hints before. The cavalry of course are the principal actors, and we are simply the supporting column.

The cavalry past us, we again started. The general hurried us up, wishing to keep as near the cavalry as possible, but the major's skirmish line rather retarded us. It was finally thought that with a large cavalry force in advance the skirmish line was not absolutely necessary, and it was withdrawn. The march was forced till past the middle of the afternoon, when it began to tell on the Brooklyn boys, some of them giving out. They were unaccustomed to such severe marching, and it took hold of them severely. We made a halt of an hour for rest and lunch, and before starting, Col. Roberts made a short address. He thought we were on the eve of a severe battle, and he hoped and believed his regiment would stand up and aquit themselves like soldiers, and if successful in our undertaking we should deserve and receive the plaudits of the country. In such a battle, there must necessarily be some victims, but just who, we are of course ignorant, but each one is hoping it will not be him. I laughed, and one of the boys asked what pleased me. I said if the colonel did not look out he would have us all whipped before we sighted the enemy. We pushed along till into the evening; the boys were getting pretty well played out and would make frequent halts without any orders.

There was one of the general's aids who seemed to take a great interest in getting us along, and his interest from some cause or other (probably his canteen) seemed to increase with the evening. The boys would be groping their weary way through the darkness, when some one would give a whistle and they would all squat in the road. This aid would ride up in a great passion and order them up, telling them if they didn't get along faster he would put a regiment of colored troops on the advance. The response to that threat would be: "Bring on your niggers!" This officer had another provoking habit which he came well nigh paying dearly for. There were occasional mud holes in the road caused by the rains; some of them two or three rods across. The boys would flank these to keep their feet from getting wet and sore, but this officer attempted to drive them through, saying it took up the time flanking them. At one of these places he was going to drive them through anyway or it would be the death of some of them. I was quietly going around, and halted to see how he made it work with them. He was swearing at them, wheeling his horse right and left among them, and making himself about as disagreeable as he could. Just then I heard the ominous click of rifle locks, and heard some one ask him if he was aware those rifles were loaded. He seemed to catch on to the idea, and got himself out of that as quickly as possible, and was seen nor heard from no more during the march. Soldiers are human, with feelings and passions like other men; they can and do stand a great deal, but they cannot stand everything any more than a stone drag.

The night wore on, the boys were well nigh exhausted and made frequent halts. The colonel would sympathize with them, and encourage them by saying he hoped the day's march was nearly over, telling them to keep up courage and a few miles more the end would be reached. At one of these halts the major showed some impatience, and riding up to the colonel said:

"Colonel, I really do not understand the meaning of this?"

"What's the matter now, major?"

"Why, every few moments this entire regiment will simultaneously sit down?"

"Oh, well, major," the colonel replied, "the boys are tired; they have come a long way and are pretty well played out; change places with some of them, major, and you will understand it better."

That seemed to be satisfactory to the major and he rode off, but it cheered the boys up wonderfully and they made quite a distance before halting again.

It is curious how sometimes the most trifling act or expression will raise up the almost exhausted energies of men and inspire hope when almost on the verge of despair. As an instance of this, the boys while marching along had for some time preserved a dead silence; not a word had been spoken, and all seemed to be absorbed in their own reflections, when suddenly I stumbled over a stump. Gathering myself up I exclaimed: "There, I know just where that stump is!" The effect was like magic; all within the sound of my voice broke out in a loud and hearty laugh, and for a time forgot their fatigue and trudged lightly along.

We reached the end of our day's tramp at New Kent, sometime after midnight, having made a march of thirty miles. Many of the boys were so exhausted that they threw themselves down on the ground and were soon fast asleep. I prepared some coffee, and while it was boiling, washed myself up, and after drinking my coffee, rolled up in my blanket and was soon asleep.

We slept about three hours when we were routed up, and a little after daylight were again on the march. The boys were pretty stiff and sore, but a mile or two took the kinks out of their legs and limbered them up so they were about as good as new. Nothing transpired worthy of note during the forenoon's march, unless it was that Capt. Phillips kept up his suppressed whistle of that same strain of Rally 'Round the Flag. I tried to rally him and get him to talking, but it was of no use; he was entirely absorbed in his own reflections, ruminating, as I thought over the probable chances of leaving a widow and orphan children as a legacy to his country.

Before noon we reached what is called the Baltimore cross roads, about two miles from Bottom bridge which crosses the Chickahominy river. Here we met the cavalry coming back, and Col. Spear reported to Gen. Wistar that on reaching the river he found all the bridges up and a considerable force of the enemy, with infantry and artillery guarding the river. With our small force and only one battery he thought it would be useless to attempt to force the passage of the river. On learning this I felt relieved, for if we couldn't cross the river to them, they certainly couldn't cross it to us, and in all probability they had no desire to do so.

Presently an alarm was raised that the enemy was coming up the White House road. The 139th was ordered down the road to meet them. We went about a quarter of a mile and formed a line of battle. A few cavalry went down the road a couple of miles and when they returned reported no enemy in sight or hearing, a circumstance I did not regret. We then went back and were dismissed for dinner.

This Baltimore is the junction of several roads; the one we came up from New Kent extends on to Richmond, one runs south to Charles City, one northeast to White House, and another runs north over into Northumberland, where once lived a little boy who owned a little hatchet and couldn't tell a lie. It was fortunate for him and the country that he lived at that time for if he had lived in these times the chances are more than a thousand to one that he couldn't have told the truth. There are some half a dozen farm houses scattered round in sight, and also the convenient blacksmith shop is located here.

In the little square formed by the intersection of the roads stands an interesting old building—the church in which Gen. Washington was married. It is a long, low, rather narrow building, without belfrey or ornament of any kind outside or in. It is without paint or even whitewash, and shows the rough marks of age and neglect. It is divested of its seats, having been used for an army hospital. I entered this historic old church and found it half full of the boys cutting their monograms in the ceiling; I uncovered my head in profound reverence for the place and the distinguished parties who were here joined in the holy bonds of wedlock. Here George and Martha mutually pledged themselves each to the other, to share together their joys and sorrows along the pathway of life until death should bring a separation, and well they kept their vows, for I have never learned that either of them ever applied for a divorce, although it is said Martha in prosperous gales was something of a shrew. For this little bit of history I am indebted to one of my Brooklyn friends who had made a previous visit here.

After waiting here a couple of hours the column re-formed and marched back over the road we came nearly to the woods, where we halted to let the cavalry go past us. After passing us they halted to feed their horses and themselves, and while waiting for them an alarm was raised that the enemy were coming through the woods on our flank. Down came the fences and a regiment of darkies filed into the field, and deployed as skirmishers. Every few moments they would look back to see where their support was, while their teeth and the whites of their eyes resembled bunches of tallow candles hanging in a dark cellar-way. The alarm of course was a false one, but the colored troops fought nobly.

We arrived back at New Kent about night, and bivouacked on a large field near the village. New Kent is the county seat, and is not much unlike other country places they call towns in Virginia. It contains a court house, jail, church, two or three stores, tavern, a small collection of houses and the inevitable blacksmith shop. There is no such thing in Virginia as a schoolhouse; they have no use for such things. All they want is law and gospel, and I have not been able to find out that these give them a great degree of culture and refinement. More than 200 years ago the colonial Gov. Berkley said: "I thank God there are no public schools in Virginia, and I hope there will be none for the next hundred years." His hopes have been doubly realized, which probably accounts for the present state of affairs in Virginia.

Getting into camp we built fires, made coffee and began to make ourselves comfortable. Some time in the evening the major happened along where a few of us were standing around a fire of burning rails. He began to upbraid us for burning the rails, telling us if we wanted fires we must go into the woods and get our fuel. I said to the major I thought it was all right to burn the rails; as we were sort of guests on the gentleman's place, I presumed he would be entirely willing and glad to contribute a few rails for our personal comfort during the night. He went off muttering something about destruction of property while the boys added more rails to the fire.

Next morning the march was resumed. Capt. Phillips came out looking bright and pert as a wildcat, the low whistle was no longer heard and he was as full of orders to his company as a major-general. We arrived back on the afternoon of the 9th, and as we sighted Camp West, the ladies were all out on the parade ground, waving their handkerchiefs in greeting of our return. It was like the old Roman armies returning from conquest, when fair maidens, with white waving arms, would welcome their coming. Now another scene ensued; fair women and brave men close in the fond embraces of love and thanksgiving for their miraculous deliverance. I could but feel that the 25th boys were rather slighted in not receiving a share of the kisses, for who can tell that but for them their friends might not now be dwellers in the Hotel de Libby. On the whole we have had rather an interesting excursion, having seen some forty odd miles of the county. It was very woody and I think the poorest I have ever traveled in for chickens, applejack and peach and honey. But the chickens and applejack didn't matter so much as the orders in regard to foraging were very strict. These officers in command here seem to think the proper way to conduct a war is not to hurt anyone or damage their property. The result was not much different from what I expected, and reminds me of the old complet:

> The king of France with 50,000 men marched up the hill
> And then marched down again.

I reckon we must have gone very near where Pocahontas befriended Capt. Smith. The history of that little romance is that Smith was captured while ascending the Chickahominy river, and taken higher up the river to Powhatan's lodge, and that was said to be some twelve miles below where the city of Richmond now stands. So I reckon we must have been in the vicinity where that occurred; I should like to have stayed there two or three days, or at least long enough to have selected some romantic spot as being the place where that drama was enacted, and if possible gathered a few stones and erected some sort of rude monument to the memory of the young lady.

Before dismissing his regiment, Col. Roberts thanked them for their cheerful obedience to orders, endurance and good order while on the march, and especially his new allies, who throughout the long march neither faltered, complained or straggled.

ALONE AGAIN.

FEB. 17. Our Brooklyn friends left us the 13th. They were ordered to report at Newport News, and we to remain here to do guard duty. When they left they expected to return in a few days, but I reckon they have gone for good, as they have sent for their ladies and quartermaster, who have gone, carrying everything with them. That leaves us alone again, and we are doing the guard duty up town, which is the outpost. It takes about one third of our men every day, and that brings us on every third day. All the camps about here are located near Fort Magruder, a large field fortification built by Gen. Magruder for the defence of Williamsburg. Since coming into Federal possession, it has been slightly altered and the guns, which formerly pointed outward, now point towards the town, about a mile distant. This was an obstacle which McClellan had to overcome in his march on Richmond. About 50 rods from its former front, now its rear, runs a wide and rather deep ravine across the country from the York to the James river, a distance of about three miles. On this line Magruder built his forts, with rifle pits in front on the edge of the ravine, for skirmishers and infantry. He had got only Fort Magruder armed on McClellan's arrival, but it proved a formidable obstacle, as it commanded the road and a wide piece of country. In front of this fort was the hottest of the battle, and not until Gen. Hancock with his corps had crossed the ravine at Queen's creek on the York river side and swooped down on Magruder's left, did he find it untenable. He then saw the day was lost and beat a hasty retreat. A few of us, while looking over the battle-ground a day or two ago, found the graves of Milford boys, who were in the 40th New York regiment.

I reckon we must have given them quite a scare up in Richmond the other day, for in the alarm and confusion which prevailed, quite a number of prisoners escaped and are finding their way in here. Yesterday the cavalry went out to assist any that might be trying to get in.

FEB. 19. We have again got somebody to look after us. Two young lieutenants have been sent here from the 148th New York at Yorktown to take command. They have taken the colonel's quarters and seem to have settled down for a good time by themselves, at any rate they don't trouble us any. They come out in the morning, and look on at guard mounting, and that is about all we see of them. I reckon they are pretty good fellows, and when I get time shall try and cultivate their acquaintance.

WILLIAMSBURG.

FEB. 22. Washington's birthday. How well Virginians have emulated his example and teachings is this day apparent. God pity the Mother of Presidents. This classic old town, next to Jamestown, is the oldest in the state. It is full of historical reminiscences and a great field for the antiquarian. Until near the close of the 17th century this was simply a suburb of Jamestown and was called the middle plantation. After the burning of Jamestown by Bacon and the accession of William III. to the throne, matters here began to assume a brighter aspect. Situated midway between the York and James rivers, which are here four miles apart, and enjoying the patronage of the king, the colonists became ambitious and thought the town would extend each way to the rivers and become the London of the New World.

For some time the founding of a college had been agitated and after the accession of William the charter was granted, he making large endowments of land and money in furtherance of the object. This was the second college in the British colonies, and in honor of the king and queen was named William and Mary. The great object of it was to educate in Virginia a succession of Church of England clergymen. After the erection of the college the town was laid out and named Williamsburg in honor of the king. From this time, under the patronage of the king and gentlemen of rank and wealth who came over and took up settlement, the town went ahead. A church, state-house and other public buildings were erected. An immense residence was built for the colonial governors and called the King James palace.

The town was the capital of the state or colony, and here the burgesses were wont to meet. It grew in population and wealth, and up to the time of the breaking out of the revolution was the most aristocratic and loyal town in all the colonies. The first thing that disturbed this truly loyal people was the debates in the house of burgesses on the stamp act, about the year 1765. Patrick Henry, then a young man and just elected to the house, opposed the act and with all his powers of reasoning and eloquence, advocated resistance to it. In these debates he gained the displeasure of some of the older members and especially those resident here. At this time Thomas Jefferson, a student in the college here, began to get interested in public affairs; he often looked in on the house of burgesses and listened to the debates, and a dozen years afterwards, in his declaration of independence, shone out the principles he there learned. Henry continued a member of the house of burgesses for several years, advocating the cause of the colonies, and in the Virginia convention to choose delegates to attend a congress of the colonies to be holden at Philadelphia to draft a declaration, he advocated it with all his impassioned eloquence, closing with those memorable words: "I know not what others may think, but as for me, give me liberty or give me death!"

About the time that Governor Gage of Massachusetts attempted to seize the stores at Concord, a similar proceeding took place here, under the direction of Lord Dunmore, the colonial governor. At midnight Capt. Collins of the armed schooner Magdalen, with a company of marines, entered the town and carried off twenty barrels of powder from the public magazine. This so incensed the people in the adjoining counties that they rose in arms and demanded a return of the powder or they would march on the town. Dunmore, becoming frightened, moved his family aboard a ship at Jamestown, and some of the leading citizens quieted the people by promising them the powder should be returned or paid for. But those promises were not kept, and Patrick Henry, at the head of about 1500 militia moved on the town, declaring he would have the powder or would make a reprisal from the public treasury. When within about fifteen miles from here he was met by a courier who paid for the powder, thus ending the expedition.

A year or two afterwards Henry was chosen governor of the colony, and on his coming here brought with him quite a force of militia. On Henry's approach Gov. Dunmore went aboard a vessel and the fleet sailed down the river. Lord Dunmore was the last colonial governor and the last occupant of the palace. Henry so hated everything that pertained to kings or royalty that he positively refused to occupy the palace, and it was left to go to decay and ruins. Nothing now remains of it save the foundations and a few scattering bricks.

WILLIAM AND MARY COLLEGE

Is now a mass of ruins; a company of the 11th Pennsylvania cavalry were the vandals. As this company were returning from a scout they were fired on with one or two shots from out the college as they were riding past. Instead of surrounding the building and capturing the murderers, they set it on fire and burned it to the ground. This college was located at the extreme western end of the town, and was a fine brick building over 100 feet in length and three stories high, with two tower entrances about 80 feet apart, in one of which was a fine bell. In front is a large park, coming to a point, forming the main entrance some 30 rods in front of the building. On each side of the gate are large live oak trees. In this park are situated four large old English style houses, two on each side and facing each other. They are about 40 feet square, two stories high, with a four-cornered roof coming to a point at the top. These were the residences of the officers and tutors of the college.

The college stands facing down the main street, which is quite a mile long; straight as a line and very wide, giving a fine view from the college. This is the second or third time that this college has been burned, but this last time seems to have been without cause or reason.

THE EPISCOPAL CHURCH,

An antiquated structure of gothic architecture, its brown spire and slender turrets pointing to where man's heart should oftener turn, is situated near the center of the town. It is built of brick brought over from England; they are very different in shape and color from those made in this country. There are no services held here now, but that doesn't matter much as it needs something more than the grace of God to keep this people in the line of duty and loyalty to the government. Their great need just at present is gunpowder. The churchyard contains over an acre, and is a cemetery where countless generations sleep forgot, and where rests his head upon the lap of earth the youth to fortune and to fame unknown.

THE OLD STATE HOUSE.

Situated not far from the church, is a plain old brick building about 60 feet long and about 30 feet wide, built on a basement story. The entrance is from a portico reached by a wide flight of steps. Here in these classic halls have been discussed grave questions of state—the destinies of the colonies, and as one walks through them, he can easily imagine he hears the voice of Patrick Henry saying: "The next gale that sweeps from the north will bring to your ears the clash of resounding arms."

THE INSANE ASYLUM

Is a large, massive, prison-looking building, filled with the unfortunate wards of the State of Virginia, but who are now the wards of the nation, and are being well and tenderly cared for. On pleasant days the mild and harmless patients have the liberty of the yard, which is spacious, well laid out and set with trees. At the entrance gates are small brick houses into which they can go when so disposed. At the gates they will stand and talk with the passers-by, asking a thousand questions and all manner of favors. Some of them are intelligent and will converse for a few minutes in a rational manner, when they will switch off on their crazy talk and lingo. This is said to be the oldest insane institution in the United States, having been founded previous to the revolutionary war, but the present building would seem to be of more recent construction.

KING JAMES' PALACE.

I have not been able to get much history of this, when or by whom it was built, and the only tradition I have been able to gather is that it was a magnificent and gorgeous establishment, where the colonial governors lived in great pomp and state. All there is left of it now is a small piece of brick work about four feet high on one of the south-west corners or angles. It was situated on the north side of the town, and back some 30 or 40 rods from the main street on which it fronted. It is difficult to form much of an idea of this building, as only the foundations are left, and a part of these are only dimly traced; but it must have been a very extensive affair. It was all of 125 feet front and 50 feet deep, with two wings in the rear extending back nearly 100 feet, leaving an open court or garden. The foundations on the front and ends show several angles, as though fashioned after some of the old English castles. The height of it can only be guessed, but probably it was not less than three stories.

The grounds and gardens which surrounded it were extensive, and must have been tastefully laid out, if one can judge by tracing the old walls, and by the few remaining shrubs and bushes which survive. The grounds in front extended to the street, making a lawn or park of some two or three acres. This has been a good deal curtailed, having been built over on three sides, leaving a common or park on the street of about an acre, called the Palace Green. Why such an establishment as this was built in this wilderness is only a matter of conjecture. It certainly was far beyond the needs of the colonial governors, and was probably built with an eye to its being a convenient refuge for royalty in case of adverse fortunes at home. Why it should have been left to decay and ruin is more than we at this day can understand. After the loyalists had left on the breaking out of the war, there probably was no one who cared enough about it to look after it, and the colonists so hated everything that pertained to royalty that it was left to the bats and owls, and in time went to ruin. Patrick Henry refused to occupy it while governor, and his successors followed his example. Egad! but what good cheer and right royal times must have been had here in those good old colony times, but the old palace to ruins has gone, leaving no memories or associations clustering around it save that it was the king's palace.

GUARD DUTY.

FEB. 27. Our guard duty is just outside the town. There are three stations: one on the south side next the asylum, one at the college on the west side, and one on the north side on the Palace Green. This last station is the one I usually take charge of. At each station the guard is divided into three reliefs, and the duty is simply to keep a lookout for the approach of the enemy and turn out the guard in honor of the officer of the day and to Col. West, the post commander. Our quarters at this station are in a small house which was formerly negroes' quarters. In the yard stands a large, unoccupied house owned by a Mr. Saunders, now a resident of New York. He is said to be a loyal man and a lawyer by profession. When McClellan passed through here, Mr. Saunders availed himself of the opportunity, and taking his family, went to New York. When I first took command of this station several mornings ago, the instructions given me were to keep a sharp lookout for the approach of the enemy. I had not been engaged in this business a great while, when the approach of Col. West was announced. I turned out the guard with a great dash, extending all the honors due his exalted rank. He inquired my instructions. I informed him of those I had received. He then inquired if I had not received instructions in regard to this house in the yard. I said I had not. "Then I will give you some; I shall expect you to look after this house and see that no one goes in there or in any way disturbs anything around it, and shall hold you responsible for its safe keeping while you are on duty." I promised to faithfully attend to that important duty. He then dismissed the guard and rode over to call on a lady friend of his.

A FRIGHTENED DARKY.

I now had a very important trust imposed on me, and I naturally felt a sort of womanly curiosity to explore that sacred realm. Soon after daylight the next morning, I took three of the boys and went around to the back side of the house and effected an entrance, but it was evident we were not the first explorers. We found nothing but a few articles of heavy furniture until we went into the southwest corner room next to the veranda. Here was a rich find, a large library. This room was about 15 feet square, and on all sides were books from the floor to the ceiling. Here was history, biography, travels, fiction, religion, law and miscellaneous works, magazines of all kinds, public documents, reports on all manner of subjects, and a large quantity of letters and private papers.

We tarried here over an hour, and on coming out met a darky on the veranda. He put on one of his ugliest looks and said:

"Wot doin' in dar? Mus keep out dar!"

"What's that to you, you black cuss?"

"You fine out, you go in dar. Colonel West tole me look out for dis yer property an' tole him wot I sees goin' on roun yere."

"And do you tell Colonel West what you see done here?"

"O, yas sah, yas sah, Ize tole him ebery ting Ize sees."

"Look here, boy, do you want to live to be old?"

"O, yas sah, yas sah."

"Well then, if you are cherishing any such desire, you must be a little careful what you say to West, for if he ever comes to us with any stories from you, we will take you out here into the woods and leave you for the buzzards to eat."

"O, lorra golly mity, boss, Ize neber ses nosin' bout de sogers, it's on'y dese yere citizens roun yere Ise looks arter, fore de Lord, boss, Ise done sa nosin bout de sogers."

"That's right, boy; you stick to that and keep it right on your mind when you see West, unless you want buzzards to your funeral."

That darky came down from boiling heat to zero in a short space of time, and as we have heard nothing from him he probably keeps the buzzards on his mind.

SALUTING THE POST COMMANDER.

A few mornings ago it was warm, sunshiny and spring-like. It was my turn on guard, and I was in command of the whole party marching through town. On the way I saw Col. West coming, and gave the order: "Shoulder arms; close up!" Just then we were passing a house on the right side of the street. On the veranda were several ladies taking their morning airing. I gave the order: "Eyes right!" West heard the order, and caught the idea; laughing, he touched his cap as he rode past us.

I reckon he was pleased with my style of soldiering as he called on me at the station a few hours afterwards. I turned out the guard and extended the customary honors. After looking us over he said:

"Sergeant, suppose you should see a force of the enemy file out of the woods over yonder, what would you do?"

"Well, sir, that would depend altogether on the size of the force."

"Well, say one or two regiments of infantry."

"In that case I should deploy my men among the buildings here, and skirmish with them until reinforcements arrived."

"Very well. Suppose a brigade of cavalry should dash out, what then?"

"In that case we would empty our rifles on them once or twice, and cut and run like hell for Fort Magruder."

"You'll do, dismiss your guard;" and wheeling his horse he rode off laughing.

SECESH LADIES.

FEB. 29. Most of the residents in town are women and small children, and a few old men. Of course the colored people are with us always. All the men being away makes society for the ladies a little one-sided. At the evacuation most of the women remained here to take care of their property, and there are very few empty houses. These ladies pretend to have a great contempt for Yankees, but still they don't appear to have quite enough to prevent their talking or chatting with us. On sunny days they may be seen at the windows or on the verandas, and a passing soldier who touches his cap in a respectful manner will perhaps get an invitation to call. If he conducts himself with propriety and is agreeable, they will ask him to be seated or perhaps ask him into the house, and on leaving, if he happens to suit them, they will invite him to call again, but some of them are not always so *agreeable* that a second call is desirable. These ladies pride themselves on being the regular F. F. V's, and have a great pride of birth and ancestry; they will sit by the hour and talk and boast of it. They claim to be the real thoroughbreds and can trace their lineage in a direct line right straight back to William and Mary.

One day, while a party of them were talking that kind of nonsense and making right smart of fun of the mixed Yankee race, I said: "So far as anything that I know to the contrary that may all be as you say, but if appearances go for anything one would naturally conclude that some of the colored people about here might boast that some of William's and Mary's blood coursed through their veins." That seemed to bring a sort of coldness over the meetin', and I began to suspect that I had seriously offended, but they soon rallied and the conversation drifted into other and more agreeable channels.

Some of the ladies are very agreeable conversationalists when they converse on something besides politics and secession, but what they say does not disturb me. I rather enjoy it, and have the fun of laughing at them. One day, in company with a party of them, they were having right smart of fun, laughing and making sport of the Yankees. I kept my end up as well as I could against such odds until they tired of it, when they switched off into secession and the war. On a table lay a small Confederate flag which one of them took up, and flaunting it around asked me how I liked the looks of it, remarking that it would finally triumph. I said that was no novelty to me, I had had the honor of helping capture quite a number of those things, "That does not represent anything, ladies; if you take any pleasure in keeping that little flag to look at occasionally as a curiosity, I presume there is no one who has the slightest objection, but be sure of one thing, you will never again see it floating in the breeze in this town."

One replied: "You seem to feel pretty secure in your holding here, but it would not take a large force of our troops to set you Yankees scampering towards Fortress Monroe."

"I know, but whatever force it might take, your people don't care to pay the cost of retaking it. Your people have too many other jobs on hand at present, and a good prospect of having more to take much trouble about this place, besides it is of no use to them anyway and but very little use to us."

Some of the women here seem to think it a mark of loyalty to their cause to exhibit all the contempt they can towards the Yankees. I fell in with a party of that kind one afternoon out in the churchyard. I sometimes go in there and spend an hour looking around and scraping the moss off those ancient stones to find names and dates, and I have found some that date back into the 17th century. In this yard are some 20 or 30 mounds beneath which sleep the Confederate dead, killed in the battle here or brought from other fields; at any rate they are here and the mounds are kept covered with flowers and evergreens. One day while looking around there a party of women entered, bringing wreaths of evergreen and commenced decorating those graves. I approached to within a respectful distance and watched them perform their sad rites of love and affection. When they had finished one of them, pointing at me, addressed me in this beautiful language: "But for you, you vile, miserable Yankees, these brave men would now be adorning their homes."

Not knowing exactly whether they would or not, or just how much of an adornment they would have been, I deemed the most fitting reply to that crazed woman was dignified silence.

CHAPTER VII.

RETURN TO NEWPORT NEWS.

MARCH 2. The 11th Connecticut regiment arrived here to-day, and we are ordered back to the News where we rejoin a part of our old regiment which has just returned from home. This is good news to our boys who have been impatiently awaiting their return. So far as I am concerned I shall leave here with some regrets. We have been here several weeks and have got used to the officers and the place. The duty is light and somebody has got to stay here; as we have only a few months longer to remain we might as well be here as anywhere; but the orders are to go and orders must be obeyed. I will call on our officers and learn more about it. I am well pleased with these young fellows. They seem to know their business and have a remarkable faculty of attending to it and letting other people attend to theirs. Their business appears to be in their quarters, amusing themselves with their reading, writing and games. They are not at all afflicted with exclusiveness and are not disposed to recline on their dignity. The boys have a standing invitation to call on them any time during office hours, and almost every evening some of them are in there. I called on them and inquired if they were going through to the News with us or stop with their regiment at Yorktown. They said it was not supposed that we knew enough to go from here to Newport News alone, and their orders were to march us down there, but they should try to get transportation from Yorktown. I said I thought that would be the most difficult job they had undertaken recently, that we could get transportation from here just as well as from Yorktown. But the idea was for us to march, as marching 50 or 100 miles a week, carrying heavy knapsacks, was a fine thing for soldiers. It took the kinks out of their legs and prevented them from becoming round-shouldered. I inquired if they thought of making the journey on brook water? One of them partly closed his left eye and replied, "Not muchly." I then said I should like an order on the commissary for a few much-needed supplies. The order was forthcoming, for which I made my best bow, and bidding them good evening took my leave.

A REUNION.

MARCH 7. Left Camp West on the 3d, arriving at Yorktown in the afternoon. Here our officers tried to get transportation but were ordered to move on. Went on about six miles below Yorktown, and on coming to an old church in the woods halted for the night. This was a brick building with nothing but the bare walls and roof, the floors, windows and finish having been removed. We gathered what wood we could find and kindled a fire inside; the night was cold and wood scarce, so that we passed a very uncomfortable night, not sleeping a wink. We took an early start in the morning, reaching the News about the middle of the afternoon, where we rejoined about 200 of the boys who first went home. We were glad to once more see each other, and the greetings were cordial among both officers and men. We introduced our new officers to our old ones, and when our new officers were about leaving us, as a slight expression of our regard for them, we shook hands with them and gave them three rousing cheers.

SNOW STORM.

MARCH 23. A snow storm commenced yesterday and continued through last night with great severity, and as our camp is only a temporary affair it afforded but slight protection; when I awoke this morning I found myself under a blanket of snow about a foot thick; there was quite a depth of snow and it was badly drifted. Before noon it cleared up and the sun shone out warm. Now commenced snow-ball battles, in which all hands engaged and seemed to take great delight. This afternoon a sleighing party drove into camp and made the rounds of the officers' quarters. This was a battery company, which out of some timbers and boards had improvised a sled about 30 feet long, and had hitched on their whole team of horses some 80 in number. The battery boys were riding the horses, while the sled was covered with officers, both military and naval. Making the rounds of the camps and being entertained at the officers' quarters, they had a high old time. It didn't matter much about the sleighing, whether good or bad, as they had team and whiskey enough to make good sleighing anywhere.

THE FAMILY TOGETHER AGAIN.

MARCH 26. Broke camp and went over to Portsmouth, opposite Norfolk. Regiment arrived in the afternoon, bringing some 250 recruits. We are once more together and the regiment now numbers about 900 men. Towards night we were ordered out to Getty's Station, about four miles west of Portsmouth.

GETTY'S STATION.

APRIL 3. This is a station on the Seaboard and Roanoke railroad; the camp ground lies between the station and the Nansemond river. The camp is named Camp Wellington in honor of a gentleman of that name in the city of Worcester, Mass., but I reckon if he could see this camp he would not feel very highly honored. It is the worst ground we have ever camped on, being little else than a mud hole. I have slept out in the woods ever since we came here, but we are getting it drained and the tents stockaded, but by the time we get it habitable we shall have to leave it.

GUERRILLA HUNTING.

APRIL 18. The country above here and that part of it lying between the Suffolk and James rivers is a good deal infected with guerrilla bands. It was thought best to send out in different directions three or four regiments to stir them up. In accordance with that arrangement we left our mud hole early in the morning of the 13th going aboard a big double-ender steamer at Portsmouth. In company with a small gunboat we steamed up the James river some 20 miles, when turning to the left we entered a small creek; following this a few miles we came to a village called Smithfield.

We landed here about noon and marched up into the street. The village seemed to be deserted, scarcely any one in sight. We had not been here many minutes before Col. Pickett was met by a good-looking elderly gentleman, who seemed to be considerably agitated about something. He wished the colonel to send a guard to his house, as he feared the negroes would take too many liberties with him during our stay. The colonel inquired if there were many Confederates about here. The old gentleman replied that he had seen none recently, and just then the report of rifles was heard up the creek. At this the colonel in a very abrupt and ungentlemanly manner, said: "D—n you and your house! Forward, march!" The old gentleman turned away sorrowfully, and started for home. This man's name was Atkinson and he was formerly a member of Congress.

A little farther up the street we made another halt to fix on some plan of action. While waiting here I went into a house. There was no one at home, but from some books and papers lying around, I learned that its occupant was a namesake of mine, a Mr. Day, a lawyer by profession. I was disappointed in not finding the 'squire at home. Mrs. Day had just finished ironing and her clothes lay on a table nice and clean. I noticed among them some towels, and being short of these, I borrowed a pair. I left my card expressing regrets at the 'squire's absence and said if he would send me his address, I should like to correspond with him.

Just out the village the roads forked. We halted a minute to determine which one to take, and while waiting a darky came along driving a pair of bulls hitched to a cart. Not being accustomed to seeing so grand a display, the animals became frightened and balked. The darky standing in the cart applied the whip and yelled at them. They began to bellow, and sticking their tails straight up in the air, went bellowing down the road at a gait which would have shamed a locomotive. We went out on the Suffolk road about five miles, where we met some scouts who said there was a regiment ahead of us. We then returned to Smithfield and soon after we were joined by the 9th New Jersey, who informed us that the 23d Massachusetts had had a brush with a party of guerrillas and had driven them towards Suffolk; those were the troops who were ahead of us when we met the scouts. The next morning on going down to the boats we saw a flag spread over something on the deck of the gunboat, and learned that it covered the body of a lieutenant of marines who was shot while going in a boat up the creek; those were the shots we heard. We arrived back to Camp Wellington in the afternoon.

A TRIP THROUGH THE CHESAPEAKE AND ALBEMARLE CANAL.

April 26. The surrender of Plymouth, N. C., and death of Flusser caused consternation at Roanoke island, lest the dreaded Albemarle should make them a visit. On the 22d we were ordered to the succor of that island. Embarking on board a large double-ender boat, we left Portsmouth in the afternoon and proceeded up the river, going past the Gosport navy yard, where could be seen the burned and sunken hulks of the U. S. vessels which were destroyed at the surrender of Norfolk and the navy yard at the beginning of the war. We kept on up the river till towards night, when we entered the canal. The boat was a little too wide for the canal and our progress was slow.

About midnight we came to a station, having made but a few miles of our journey. There we found our Brooklyn friends who were doing picket duty. They were right glad to see us and kept us busy answering questions about their old home, which they were beginning to despair of ever seeing again. After an hour's stop we resumed our journey. We had not gone far when the port wheel fouled with a stump, so that we could neither go ahead nor back off. This caused a delay of about two hours, as cutting out floats by the light of a lantern is a slow job. A mile or so further on a similar accident happened. This time they went to work cutting out the stump which was of considerable size, and took with a large amount of swearing, until after daylight to get clear. The port wheel had now acquired a provoking habit of fouling with all the stumps and snags along the bank, and not until late in the afternoon of the 23d did we come out to a lake, sound, bay, or at any rate a large sheet of water, which we crossed, and just before night again entered the canal.

We now enter the eastern edge of the great dismal swamp. I have sometime read a legend of the phantom or witch of the lake of the dismal swamp, who all night long, by the light of the firefly lamp, would paddle her light canoe. On each side of the canal is a cypress swamp, and as the officers were about retiring for the night in the house on deck, the colonel charged the boys to keep a sharp lookout for guerrillas and bushwhackers who

might be lurking there. About midnight all was still, not a
sound was heard save the dull, heavy wheezing of the engines.
Stripped of their bark, the dead trunks of the cypress trees
looked in the dim light of the sweet German silver-plated moon,
weird and ghostlike. Now it required no great stretch of the imagination to see almost anything in this swamp, and it began to
be whispered around that bushwhackers could be seen behind the
trees. Presently the sharp crack of a rifle rang out on the still
night air, followed by a general fusillade and a cry that the woods
are full of them. The officers came rushing out of the house and
the colonel strained his eyes peering into the swamp, but seeing
nothing and hearing no return fire, he naturally concluded that
the boys were drawing on their imaginations, and gave the order
to cease firing. But in such a racket it was difficult to hear orders, especially if they didn't care to, and before he got them
stopped, he was giving his orders in very emphatic language. It
was rare sport to see the firing go on and to hear the colonel trying to stop it.

About morning we entered the North river, coming out into
Currituck sound and sailing around the head of the island, landed
at old Fort Unger. The garrison consisted of only the 99th New
York, who felt a little nervous about being caught here alone in
case the Albemarle should make them a visit. On landing we
learned the scare was all over. The ram left Plymouth, intending to come here, but on getting out into the sound the old ferry-
boats which had been lying in wait went for her and came well
nigh sinking her; at any rate they disabled her so much she put
back to Plymouth. Finding we were not needed here, after a
few hours' rest we re-embarked and started back.

The next day as we came out into the wide sheet of water, a
cry was raised: "Sail ho! Sail ho!" "Where away?" "Five
points off the port bow." And sure enough, a little to the left
and nearly across this lake, sound or whatever it is, lay a small
steamer, which proved to be the little mail-boat Gazelle, which
lay there stranded. We hauled up and inquired if they wished
any assistance. They replied they should be all right as soon as
the sand washed from under them, but in the meantime would
like a guard aboard. About a dozen men from Company A were
put aboard and we went on, arriving back to camp late last evening.

YORKTOWN.

MAY 3. On the 27th of April we broke camp at Getty's station, arriving here about dark, and marched up the Williamsburg
road about two miles where we bivouacked. On this trip we
were furnished transportation. On the morning of the 29th we
were ordered into camp about three miles higher up the road.
We had not much more than got up there when an order came

for us to report at the landing immediately. We now had a five mile march before us, with the dust in the road about three inches deep. This was no march but a race, the companies trying to run past each other and get the advance to shield themselves from the dust. The colonel let them have it their own way and they made the dust fly right smart. We made the distance in less than an hour and on arriving at the landing looked like walking dirt heaps. A guard was placed along the bank of the river to prevent our washing in it for fear of creating a sand bar. There didn't appear to be anything wanted of us after we got here and we are now in camp on the bluff just above the landing.

Our brigade now consists of the 9th New Jersey and the 23d, 25th and 27th Massachusetts, under command of Brig. Gen. C. A. Heckman, and is known as the 1st brigade, 2d division, 18th army corps, under command of Gen. William F. Smith, otherwise known as "Baldy." Our knapsacks have been sent back to Portsmouth and we are now in light marching order, having only the clothing we have on and our blankets. Our camp equipage consists of two camp kettles for each company, and shelter tents. These tents are simply pieces of cotton cloth, about six feet long by four wide, made to button together, and every man is supplied with one which he carries with his blanket. Ordinarily they are used as blankets, but in case of a storm three of them are buttoned together, two forming the roof and the other the end, which makes a kind of burrow which partly shelters three men. We fellows who are used to roughing it think it all well enough, but I feel sorry for the officers ; it will come pretty hard on them. It is something they are not used to and besides it sort of reduces them to the ranks.

Yorktown is hardly as much today as it was the day of Cornwallis' surrender, and I don't think there has been a nail driven or an ounce of paint used since. There is the old church and about a dozen weather-beaten old houses, the most pretentious of which was Cornwallis' headquarters.

The 18th corps are all here, infantry, artillery and cavalry, and yesterday Gen. Butler reviewed them. The review came off on the plain below the town and was quite an imposing affair. We came a very clever little dodge on the enemy last night. About midnight we were all routed up and every man given a chunk of raw salt pork. After standing there about half an hour holding our pork and awaiting further developments, we were then told we might go back to bed again. Now that was taking a mean advantage of a brave and chivalrous foe, thus to conceal the kind and quantity of our rations. They are probably thinking that we have nothing to eat and are keeping up their hopes that we shall soon surrender.

WE LEAVE YORKTOWN.

MAY 8. On the afternoon of the 4th we went aboard the boats and dropped anchor at Fortress Monroe at dusk. The next morning we started up the James river. The river was alive with boats, schooners, tugs, gunboats, monitors and everything that could float, all loaded to their fullest capacity with troops, horses, artillery and all the paraphernalia of war. We passed Jamestown in the afternoon. Nothing now remains to mark the spot where the first settlement in Virginia was made, but a pile of bricks which composed a part of one of the buildings. We reached City Point just before night. Gen. Heckman's brigade landed on the Bermuda Hundred side and bivouacked a short distance from the landing, all the other troops remaining aboard the boats. The gunboats and monitors commenced fishing for torpedoes and working their way up the James and Appomatox rivers.

The next morning, the 6th, the troops commenced to land and Heckman's brigade was ordered to advance. We marched up the country six or seven miles, getting on to high ground and what is called Cobb's Hill. From here the spires of the churches in Petersburg can be seen, while in front of us is a kind of valley. At this point the Appomatax river turns in a southwesterly direction. On the banks between us and Petersburg was a battery. This is called a good position and here we halted. We sat here under a burning sun, watching the long lines of troops come up and file off to the right into the woods towards the James river until past the middle of the afternoon, at which time the whole of the 18th and 10th corps, comprising the army of the James, under Gen. B. F. Butler, had arrived.

HECKMAN'S BRIGADE LEADS OFF THE DANCE.

About 4 p. m., Gen. Heckman is ordered to make a reconnoisance towards the Petersburg and Richmond railroad. We moved down the valley in a southwesterly direction, and when about three miles out the 27th Massachusetts were advanced as skirmishers. A mile or two farther on we began to hear scattering shots, indicating that our skirmishers had found game. We hurried on and found the enemy in a shallow cut, on a branch railroad running from Port Walthal to the Petersburg and Richmond road. A sharp skirmish ensued, lasting till near dark, when Heckman withdrew, having accomplished his purpose of finding the enemy. In this skirmish the 25th lost four killed and several wounded.

The next morning, the 7th, we moved on them in force, Gen. Brooks' division moving directly on the Petersburg and Richmond railroad. Heckman's brigade, with a section of a battery, were ordered to occupy the ground of the night before. The enemy were in strong force and opened on us with artillery. Heckman paid no attention to that, but moved his battalions into line on the field in columns by division, and ordered them to lie down. The 25th were partially covered by a slight roll of ground in our front, while the 27th Massachusetts on our left were badly exposed to the enemy's fire and were suffering severely. Heckman saw the situation and ordered Col. Lee to move his regiment to the rear of us. He then ordered forward his artillery, placing them in battery in our front and set them to work. They made the rail fences and dust fly right smart. After a few shots had been fired a loud explosion was heard, followed by a big cloud of smoke, dust and debris in the enemy's line. One of their caissons had blown up, and our boys rose up and gave rousing cheers. Our guns continued shelling them, but got no return fire, their ammunition was probably exhausted and their guns perhaps disabled.

There was no infantry firing on either side, we simply holding our line and watching events. Heavy firing was heard over on the railroad. Brooks was at them and a fight for the railroad was going on. We were masters of the situation here and were able to protect his flank. About noon the enemy got an old gun into position and commenced throwing chunks of railroad iron at us. This caused considerable sport among the boys and they would cheer them lustily every time they fired, but a few shots from our guns, put a quietus on that sport. I have often read and heard of that kind of practice, but never saw any of it until now.

In the afternoon a battery of four 20-pounder parrott guns drove up, taking positions on a roll of ground some 20 rods in our rear and commenced firing. I at first thought they were shelling the enemy in front of us, and was a little surprised at it as all was quiet on both sides. But I soon noticed they were not. I got permission from Capt. Emery and went up there. Here was a signal officer, and nearly half a mile away to the northwest was a group of men signaling to this battery. The guns were at quite an elevation, and they would train them a little to the right or left, as directed by the signal officer. They were throwing shells over the woods and dropping them among the enemy over on the railroad, some two miles away. Those shells were reported to be very annoying to the enemy and of great service to Brooks. It was splendid artillery practice and I was greatly interested in it. While watching them shy those shells over the woods I wondered where those devils over there thought they came from.

Towards night it was signaled that Brooks had accomplished his purpose, tearing up several miles of road and was drawing back to our line. The day's work was over and we drew back to Cobb's Hill. In this day's fight the 27th Massachusetts sustained the greatest loss, while the 25th suffered the worst in last night's affair. The heat was intense, and the men suffered severely, many of them being prostrated and carried back in ambulances.

ON THE SICK LIST.

MAY 18. Since the affair over on the railroad, I have been on the sick list and have suffered severely with chills and fever and from other causes. I am not yet able to do much and I fear I shall not be able to go on many more excursions with the boys. The regiment has been out nearly every day, and has suffered a loss of more than 200 men, killed, wounded and prisoners. In the fight at Drury's Bluff, two mornings ago, we lost heavily, some 150 men being killed, wounded or taken prisoners. Heckman's brigade was almost annihilated. He was taken prisoner together with Capt. Belger, who lost four pieces of his battery, and Col. Lee, with nearly the whole of the 27th Massachusetts regiment, besides a good many officers and men of the 23d Massachusetts and 9th New Jersey.

18TH CORPS HOSPITAL, POINT OF ROCKS, SUNDAY, JULY 10, 1864. I have been here a little more than a week and begin to feel a little rested. I have not written a letter for more than a month and about everything has been neglected. I hung around the regiment as long as Ass't Surgeon Hoyt would allow me to, and the first of the month he piled me into an ambulance and sent me here, saying I could have a much better celebration here than I could in the trenches. This was my first ride in an ambulance and I didn't enjoy it worth a cent. I have always had a strong aversion to that kind of conveyance and have always clung to the hope that I might be spared from it. My health began to fail early in the spring. I said nothing about it, thinking I should improve as the weather grew warmer, but instead of improving I grew worse, until now I am unfit for anything. At first I was terribly afflicted with piles, then chills and fever, and now I have a confirmed liver complaint which no amount of blue mass, calomel or acids affect in the least unless it is to help it along. I reckon if I can keep pretty quiet and can hold out till I get home I shall stand a chance to recover from it, but it will be a slow job.

HOSPITAL LIFE.

JULY 20. Thus far I have been unable to discover any charms in hospital life. With fair health the active camp is far preferable. This hospital is divided into three departments. The first is the officers' ward, the second is the hospital for the wounded and very sick, and the third is the convalescent camp. The first two are in large hospital tents and are furnished with cots, mattresses and other necessary conveniences. In the third are more than 600 men, quartered under shelter tents. I am in this department. It is not supposed that there are any sick men here. They are all either dead beats or afflicted with laziness, and a draft is made from among them twice a week for the front. I had been here only four days when I was drawn, but Garland of company C, who is an attache at Doctor Sadler's office, saw my name on the roll and scratched it off. Although there are none here supposed to be sick, there seems to be a singular fatality among them as we furnish about as large a quota every day for the little cemetery out here as they do from the sick hospital. But then in a population of 600 or more, three or four deaths a day is not surprising. I have been here three weeks and have been drafted four times, but with my friend Garland's help I have escaped. I should be pleased to be back with the boys if I was only half well, but I reckon I shall not be troubled with any more drafts. Doctor Hoyt sent a man back the other day. The next morning he was sent up with a sharp note to Doctor Sadler, saying that he didn't send men to the hospital that were fit for duty and didn't want them sent back until they were. That roused Doctor Sadler's ire, and he says when Hoyt wants his men he can send for them.

Doctor Sadler has the whole charge of the convalescent camp, and has several young fellows, assistant surgeons so called, on his staff. Some of these fellows I should think had been nothing more than druggists' clerks at home, but by some hook or crook have been commissioned assistant surgeons and sent out here. Every morning all who are able in all the ten wards go up to be examined and prescribed for by these new fledged doctors, and those not able to go seldom receive any medical attendance, but it is just as well and perhaps better that they do not go, as the skill of these young doctors is exceedingly limited. Doctor Sadler is a fine man and a skilful surgeon. He comes around occasionally, visiting those who are not able to go out and prescribes for them, and for a day or two afterwards the assistants will attend to those cases. These assistants make the examinations and draft the men for the front, after which they are again examined by Doctor Sadler and frequently a number of them will not be accepted, and the assistants oftentimes need not feel very much flattered by some remarks of the doctor.

This convalescent camp holds its own in spite of all the drafts made on it. Recruits arrive daily and the drafts are made twice a week, sending back 50 or 100 at each draft. When a draft is made one of the assistants comes into a ward and orders it turned out, and every man not down sick abed turns out. The ward-master forms them in single rank and the inspection begins. They commence on the right and go through the ward, making the same examinations and asking the same questions of every man in the ward. They feel the pulse and look at the tongue, and if those are right they are booked for the front. They remind me of horse jockeys at Brighton, examining horses. Some of the boys who are well enough but are in no hurry to go back, chew wild cherry or oak bark to fur their tongues and are thus exempted until Doctor Sadler gets hold of them, when they have to go. We get some recruits from the other hospital, for as soon as a sick or wounded man there is declared convalescent he is sent here.

A good joke occurred one morning when one of them was drafted for the front. He had been slightly wounded in the leg and was getting around with a crutch. When his ward was ordered out for draft he fell in with the rest, and the doctor, not noticing the crutch, but finding his pulse and tongue all right, marked him as able-bodied. When Sadler inspected them, he said to this fellow: "What are you here for?" "Going to the front, I suppose; there is where I am ticketed for." Sadler laughed, and said: "I'll excuse you." Then turning to his assistant, remarked: "We are not yet so hard up for men as to want three-legged ones." That assistant looked as though he wished he was at home under his mother's best bed.

This whole hospital is under the management of a Doctor Fowler, and as far as I am able to judge is well and skilfully managed. The cuisine is excellent and far better than could be expected in a place like this. The hospital fund as fast as it accrues is expended for vegetables, fruits, milk, butter, cheese, preserves and many other things which the government is not supposed to furnish. The kitchen is in two departments, one where are cooked and served out the meats, soups, vegetables and other food for the convalescent. In the other are cooked the roasts, steaks, broths, beef tea and* all kinds of light diet for the officers' ward and the sick and wounded department. The light diet is presided over by an angel of mercy in the person of a Miss Dame who is the hospital matron.

I RECEIVE AN APPOINTMENT.

August 1. The ward next me on the left is a colored one, and contains from 60 to 80 men, according to recruits and drafts. Until recently they have been pretty much on their own hook, no one seeming to care for them. Some days ago Doctor Sadler asked me if I would take charge of them. I said I should like to do anything where I could be of any use. He gave me my instructions and some blank reports, and set me up in business. My duties are to attend roll-calls, surgeon's calls, keep an account of arrivals, discharges, desertions, deaths, march them up to the kitchen three times a day for rations and make my report to him every morning. Entering on the discharge of my duties the first thing I did was to set them to work cleaning and fixing up their quarters, so they would be more comfortable.

A couple of hours' work showed a great improvement in the condition of things, and while it was being done it gave me a chance to find out who among them were the worst off and needed the most care and favors. A sick nigger is a curious institution and you can't tell so well about him as you can about a sick mule. He can put on the sickest look of anything I ever saw and appear as though he would die in seven minutes, but a nigger is never really sick but once, and is then sure to die. There is no more help for one than there is for a sick pig. I have three that are sick and I have no more faith in their getting well than I have that Gen. Lee will drive Gen. Grant from before Petersburg. Two of them are now unable to attend the surgeon's call in the morning and the other I expect will be in a few days. I have about 40 hobbling around with canes, spavined, ring-boned and foundered. The others are simply a little war-worn and tired.

The kitchen is about 30 rods from the camp, and when I march them up there there are so many lame ones they straggle the whole distance. Doctor Sadler called my attention to this and said he should like to see them march in little better order. I replied: "Surgeon, come out in the morning and see the parade; you will see them marching a 28 inch step and closed up to 18 inches from stem to stern." He promised he would. The next morning at breakfast call I formed every one of those darkies that carried canes on the right, and the very lamest I put at the head of the column, and gave them a send-off. It was a comical show, they marched at the rate of about one mile an hour, and those in the rear kept calling out to those in advance: "Why don ye goo long dar! Hurry up dar; shan' get breakfas' fo' noon." They kept closed up a good deal better than they kept the step as the rear crowded the advance to push them along. We were cheered along the route as almost everybody was out to see the fun. We marched in review before the doctor, and by the way he laughed and shook himself I thought he was well satisfied with the parade, at any rate he complimented me on my success when I carried in my morning report.

One day one of my fellows came to me for a pass to go fishing. He said he could catch as many bull-heads as would do us two for three days. I gave him a pass, but didn't see anything of him again for four days. When I asked him where he had been so long, he looked pretty sober for a minute or two, and then rolling around the whites of his eyes and showing his teeth, said: "Yah, yah, yah! ize no idee ize don gon so long; yah, yah, yah."

NED CARTER THE BLACKSMITH.

August 8. When I first came here I was pretty well used up, but thanks to my friends, Garland of company C and Wheelock and Aldrich of my own company (who are attaches of this hospital), and also to Miss Dame for their attention, kindness and favors, I am feeling the best now I have any time this summer. For their sympathy, attentions and kind offices, I am under a debt of everlasting gratitude.

Within a week two of my sick men have died and another is fast going. One of them was a character in his way. As near as one can guess the age of a darky I should judge he was about 60 years old, and rather an intelligent man. He always called himself Ned Carter the blacksmith, and delighted in having others call him so. He would talk by the hour of old times, about his old master, and the good times and good cheer they used to have at Christmas time. When I first took this ward I saw that Ned was a sick darky and told him to have things his own way; if he felt like sleeping in the morning and didn't want to come out to roll call I would excuse him. I noticed that he seldom went for his rations, but would send his cup for his coffee and tea. He said there was very little at the kitchen he could eat. I asked him what he could eat. He said he thought some cracker and milk would taste good. I took his cup up to Miss Dame and asked her if she would give me some condensed milk and a few soda crackers for a sick darky. She gave them to me, and Ned Carter the blacksmith was happy. The convalescent camp is not allowed anything from the sick kitchen, except by order of Doctor Fowler, so any little notion I get from there is through the kindness of Miss Dame or my friend Wheelock. I have often carried Ned a cup of tea and a slice of toast, with some peach or some kind of jelly on it, and the poor fellow could express his gratitude only with his tears, he had no words that could do it. One morning after roll call I went to his little tent and called Ned Carter the blacksmith. I got no response, and thinking he might be asleep I looked in. Ned Carter the blacksmith was gone, but the casket that had contained him lay there stiff and cold.

THE CHRISTIAN AND SANITARY COMMISSIONS.

August 20. I have read a great deal in the papers of the Christian and Sanitary commissions, of the noble and humane work they were doing and the immense amount of money contributed for their support by the people throughout the north and west. I have taken a great interest in these commissions and have supposed they were a kind of auxiliary to the medical and surgical department of the army, carrying and dispensing some simple medicines, pouring in the balm of gilead and binding up gaping wounds, giving comfort and consolation to the sick, weary and distressed; but in all this, so far as my observation has gone, I find I have been laboring under a delusion. Since I have been here is the first I have ever seen of the workings of these commissions, and I have watched them with some interest and taken some pains to find out about them. Here is a branch of each, located midway the convalescent camp and sick hospital, and I find they are little else than sutler's shops, and poor ones at that. These places are said to furnish without money and without price to the inmates of this hospital and the boys in the trenches such little notions and necessities as we have been accustomed to buy of the sutlers, and in consequence of this no sutlers are allowed to locate anywhere in this vicinity. The boys are not supposed to be fooling away their money to these thieving sutlers when our folks at home are willing to supply our little needs, free gratis for nothing. So when we happen to want a lemon or a pencil, a sheet of paper or a piece of tobacco, or whatever other little notion we require, all we have to do is to apply to one or the other commission and make known our wants; after answering all the questions they are pleased to ask we are given a slice of lemon, a half sheet of paper or a chew of tobacco. These are not wholesale establishments.

Fortunately for me I have stood in very little need of anything within their gift. I seldom solicit any favors and those are granted so grudgingly I almost despise the gift. My first experience with these institutions was one day when I was out of tobacco, I called on the Christians and told them how I was situated. I got a little sympathy in my misfortunes and a short lecture on the sin of young men contracting such bad habits, when I was handed a cigar box containing a small quantity of fine cut tobacco and told to take a chew. I asked them if they couldn't let me have a small piece that would do me for a day or two. "Oh, no; that is not our way of doing business." "Will you sell me a piece? I would as soon buy of you as of the sutler." "Oh no; it is against our orders to sell anything. All there is here is free, it costs you nothing." He then put up a small quantity and gave me. The next day I sent down to the Point and bought some. My next call was for a pencil. I was handed a third of one. I said if that is the best you can do perhaps you had better keep it. He then gave me a whole one. I got out of writing paper and thought I would beg some. I called for it, and was given a half sheet. I used that and went for more, and when I had finished my letter, I had been six times to the Christian's. I sent down to the Point and bought some. I sometimes think I should like a lemon, but there is poor encouragement for calling for one, as I notice that others calling for them only get a thin slice of one.

This is the first place I ever got into where I could neither buy, steal nor beg. I notice the officers fare a little better; they get in fair quantity almost anything they call for. I sometimes stand around for an hour and watch the running of this machine and wonder that in this business of giving goods away where the necessity for lying comes in, and yet I notice that this is practiced to some extent. Sometimes a person calling for an article will be told they are out of it, but expect some when the team come up from the Point. In a little while after perhaps some officer will call for the same thing and get it.

This Christian commission seems to be the headquarters for visitors. They stay a few days, going as near the trenches as they dare to, and in the chapel tent in the evening will tell over their adventures and pray most fervently for the boys who hold them. We are never short of visitors, as soon as one party goes, another comes, and they all seem to be good Christian men, taking great interest in the welfare of our souls.

A CHARACTER.

Among our visitors is a tall, lean, middle-aged man whom I know must have seen right smart of trouble. His face is snarled and wrinkled up in such a way that it resembles the face of a little dog when catching wasps. Although there is no benevolent expression on his countenance, he yet has more sympathy to the square inch than any other man I ever saw. He takes a great interest in this convalescent camp and seems to have taken it under his special charge. He will be in this camp all day, calling on all hands, inquiring after their health and needs, praying with them, giving them sympathy and good advice. He will come round giving a thin slice of lemon to all who will take it, and will sometimes go through the camp with a basket of linen and cotton rags and a bottle of cologne, sprinkling a little on a rag and give it to any one who will take it and at the same time will distribute religious tracts. Some days he will come round with a bottle of brandy and some small lumps of sugar, on which he will drop three or four drops of the brandy and give it to any one who says they are troubled with bowel complaints, at the same time telling them he hopes it will do them good.

One day he came along distributing temperance tracts. He looked into my tent and inquired if there were any objections to his leaving some. I replied there were no reasons known to exist why he might not leave all he wished to. I then said: "You are laboring in a very worthy cause, but you seem to be working the wrong field, or as Col. Crockett used to say, barking up the wrong tree, for we here might just as well cast our nets into the lake that burns with fire and brimstone, thinking to catch speckled trout as to think of getting any liquor. Your field of labor would seem to be up in the officers' ward where you deal out your liquors." The old gentleman sighed at such perverseness and went along. He will work this camp all day from early morning till night, giving every one something, and in all that time will not give away the value of fifty cents.

Now I don't wish to cast any reflections or create any false impressions in regard to these commissions. I have only written *my* experience and observations as to their workings in this convalescent camp. So far as anything that I know to the contrary, they may be doing a great and humane work in the wounded and sick hospital, and I am charitable enough to allow that they are, but if the whole system of it throughout the army is conducted as niggardly as I have seen it here then there must be some superb lying done by somebody to account for all the money that is being contributed for its support.

I REJOIN MY REGIMENT.

SEPT. 2. About a week ago my brigade, Gen. Stannard commanding, left the trenches and was ordered into camp at Cobb's Hill; all the convalescents belonging to it were ordered to rejoin it. When I was about leaving, all my darkies gathered around me to give me their blessing and say their goodb-yes. They were earnest in their thanks for the kind treatment they had received and expressed their regrets at my leaving them. I told them to be good boys and do their duty, and they would surely receive their reward. It is possible the poor devils will miss me, as I have been to them not only ward-master, but doctor, nurse and attendant. I think I have been very successful with them in the little time I have had charge of them, having lost by death only three and I think there is small chance of any more of them dying at present, unless they should happen to be struck by lightning.

Our brigade musters scarcely 1000 men for duty, and in a few weeks will be still further reduced by the expiration of the terms of service of those not re-enlisting. I learn that in a few days we go to Newbern, N. C., to relieve a full brigade which is ordered up here. Our old lines here are now nothing more than skirmish lines on either side, with a few pickets between. There is no firing from either side, and all is still and quiet as Sunday. The pickets keep up a truce between themselves, and although against orders, trading and communicating are carried on between them. I called on my old friend Lieut. McCarter of company B. He is now on Gen. Stannard's staff, and is serving as brigade commissary, which gives him a fine opportunity to entertain his friends. It has been several months since I saw Mac, but he is the same genial, good-natured fellow as ever. Of course our greetings were cordial. He says the job is more to his liking than dodging shell at Cold Harbor, and the only disagreeable thing about it is in lugging water to make his accounts balance.

WE LEAVE VIRGINIA.

NEWBERN, SEPT. 15. On the 5th of this month the 23d and 25th Massachusetts embarked on the steamer Winona, from Bermuda Hundred bound for Newbern. The 9th New Jersey and 27th Massachusetts embarked on another boat at the same time for the same destination. On the morning of the 6th we ran up to Portsmouth, taking our camp equipage and knapsacks aboard, and ran back into Hampton Roads and anchored. There was a heavy storm blowing outside and we lay at our anchorage all day the 7th. On the 8th we steamed up and anchored off Fortress Monroe, but soon received orders to put out to sea. The captains of both boats objected to going, saying it was too rough to venture outside. On the morning of the 9th we received peremptory orders to pull up our mudhooks and start. Then ensued a sharp correspondence between our captain and some one in the fort, said to be Gen. Butler, and it certainly sounded a great deal like him. The captain objected to taking out his boat on the ground that she was only a light river boat and entirely unfit for an ocean trip, and besides was only chartered for the bay and rivers, and he did not feel like taking her out without first consulting her owners at Baltimore. Word came back that it made no difference about the owners or for what she was chartered, the boat was going to Newbern or go to pieces. In this dilemma the captain said that the boat might go but that he shouldn't take the responsibility of taking her out. Soon word came back that he *would* take her out, or go into the fort, wearing a ball and chain. The captain, finding himself of no more account than a common soldier, was obliged to accept the situation. Toward night our consort, which was a sea-going boat, led off, we following after.

I felt a little nervous about going out to sea in so frail a craft, and thought it rather rough that after having gone through what we had we should be taken out to sea and drowned. I comforted myself with the thought that soldiers were not supposed to have any choice in the manner of their death. We found it rough going round Cape Henry, as there is almost always a chop sea there even in mild weather. Getting around the cape, we encountered heavy swells and rollers and every little while a big roller would strike us under the port guard and make every timber in the old craft snap. I expected every minute to see the guard, if not the whole deck torn off. I remained awake the whole night watching our consort, which kept just ahead of us, and reckoned on my chance for a swim.

We reached Hatteras inlet early on the morning of the 10th, and landed at Fort Spinola, on the south side of the Trent river at Newbern, in the afternoon. After landing we marched up into the camp of the 9th Vermont—a sick, ragged, dirty, lousy crowd. The Vermonters gathered wonderingly around us, extending us every sympathy and hospitality that lay in their power. The old regiment was divided off into three or four small companies, one of which under command of Capt. Emery, was sent out to Price's creek, about a mile from here, to go into quarters and do some light picket duty. We have once more got ourselves cleaned up, our hair trimmed and dressed in clean, whole clothing, and begin to look quite like ourselves again.

We are again on our old stamping ground, but, alas, how changed! Only a small remnant now remains of that grand old regiment that left Worcester three years ago. They fill honored graves on half a hundred battlefields, they are inmates of every hospital from Boston to Newbern, and are wasting away in rebel prisons; a handful only remaining to tell the sad tale. In a few days more they will be still further decimated by a hundred or more whose time will be out and go home. The whole south for the past three years has been singularly exempt from the scourge of yellow fever, but it has now broken out in Newbern, and is raging to a great extent, 30 or 40 dying daily. It has not yet reached the camps outside the city, and hopes are entertained that it will not.

OFF FOR HOME.

On the 5th of October, two days before the expiration of our term of service, an order came to Price's creek, ordering all those who were entitled to muster out to turn over to the proper authorities our arms and equipments and report at the railroad station near Fort Spinola. This was just after dinner. Capt. Emery sent to the pickets across the creek for all those who had not re-enlisted to report at quarters. In a few minutes we were all there; the captain read the order and the boys cheered. I was all ready to comply with the order, and bidding faithful Spitfire a long and final farewell, I handed it to the captain. It was soon found out what was up, and for the next half hour the enemy was left to take care of themselves, and all hands gathered at quarters to say their good-byes and see us off. We went aboard the cars at Fort Spinola and picked up others along the road, arriving at Morehead about dusk. There about 100 of us went aboard the steamer Dudley Buck, and soon after were sailing out the harbor of Beaufort, leaving behind us the scenes of our triumphs and hardships. The next morning we were around Cape Lookout and out to sea. Pretty soon we saw the officers come up out of the cabin, they were talking among themselves and seemed to wear a troubled look. It was soon discovered that there was a lot of citizens aboard coming down with yellow fever, and before noon one was brought up out of the cabin dead and laid in a boat that hung on the davits.

AN INDIGNATION MEETING.

The boys held an indignation meeting, declaring it was wrong and cruel on the part of the government or other authorities to allow these men to come aboard, and it seemed to be the evident intent of the government or some one else to murder us. They had just tried to drown us and failing in that had now, after having gone through one of the most unheard of campaigns, and as though were too obstinate to die, would give us one more chance, and smuggle aboard a lot of yellow fever stricken devils to go home with us. The captain disclaimed all knowledge of how they came aboard, but it was evident they were here and couldn't have got here without the knowledge and consent of somebody. They still further declared that those citizens were of no earthly use nor hadn't been of any, they were simply buzzards who had run away from the draft in New York, and were now running away from the yellow fever, and as a measure of safety and self-protection it was voted to throw them all overboard. The captain thought that would be most too summary a way of disposing of them, besides we would be liable to a charge of mutiny and murder at sea. It certainly was no lack of will, but only our better judgment that prevented their being thrown overboard. We reached Fortress Monroe on the forenoon of the 7th and were detained several hours by some quarantine regulations, but were finally permitted to resume our journey.

IN QUARANTINE.

On the morning of the 9th we sighted Sandy Hook, and on getting nearer we could see quite a fleet of vessels lying there. This was the lower quarantine. We ran through this, arriving at the upper quarantine at Staten Island about 10 a. m. We were now in sight of New York, and were buoyant in hope that we should soon be there. As we neared a big steamer lying in the middle of the channel we were hailed with "Steamer ahoy!" We slowed down and ran alongside. Some kind of an official came to the middle gangway and said:

"Where are you from?"
"Beaufort, North Carolina."
"Any sick aboard?"
"Yes, sir."
"Any deaths?"
"Yes, sir."
"How many days out?"
"Four."

"How many deaths?"

"Four."

"Four deaths in four days. About ship and go back to the Hook."

Our hearts that a few moments before were buoyant with hope now sank within us. The Hook was a cold, dreary place, and there was no knowing how long we should have to stay, but it was easy enough to know that some of us wouldn't stay there very long. We ran back to the Hook, and dropped anchor, not far from the large hospital ship.

After a little while we saw a gig lowered from the hospital ship; a man stepped in and was pulled alongside our boat; he climbed aboard and proved to be some kind of health officer. He looked us all over and then looked over the boat. He signaled a tug to run alongside, he hustled out those citizens, and put them aboard of it. He also took Samuel Champney of company D, whom he found lying down, and took them all over to the hospital ship. We bade Sam good-bye as he went over the side of the boat. We never saw him afterwards, and I have since learned that he died there. The next morning, when the gig was seen coming over, the call went over the boat: "All hands on deck; don't be caught lying down; all out on deck!" When he came aboard he found us all fooling and knocking off caps. He looked us over and remarked that we didn't seem to be ailing very much. He then looked the boat over and not finding any down took his leave, but if he could have looked through the side of the boat he would have seen half of us down by the time he was in his gig.

Capt. Denny of company K, who is in command of this detachment, and who is a genial, big-hearted man, said he would see what he could do for us. He went over to the hospital ship and a little while after we saw him on a tug going towards New York. I knew if there was any help for us, Capt. Denny was the man to do it. He is a good talker and great in diplomacy, and when he sets about a thing he is pretty sure to accomplish something. Tuesday night came but no Denny, and the question, "Where is Denny?" was oft repeated without an answer. I could but feel that the captain was working for us and no news was perhaps good news. Wednesday morning, the 12th, was a cold, bleak, cheerless morning, and we were growing weaker every hour, but all hands rallied on deck when that hospital fiend was seen coming. Noon came but no Denny. Where is Denny? What has happened to him? Can it be possible that he has deserted us? were questions that went unanswered. I said it was possible something may have happened to him, but I *cannot* believe he has deserted us. He is not that kind of a man, besides he would not miss taking us into Worcester for half the wealth of the city, but if he don't come tonight, we will send Captains Parkhurst and Emery to see what has become of him.

About 3 p. m. we sighted a large tug coming through the narrows, and soon after it headed towards our boat. Long before it got within hail we saw a man in the bow, waving his cap. It was Capt. Denny. Deliverance had come, and I reckon when that hospital doctor heard our cheers, he must have thought we were not very badly affected with yellow fever. I had known Capt. Denny for several years before the war, but cannot remember a time when I was so glad to see him as I was on that afternoon. The tug came alongside and we were not very long transferring ourselves aboard of it and it was again heading for the city. We ran along the starboard side of the Norwich steamer, and boarded her at the forward gangway, and were hustled among the cotton bales and freight like so many lepers. We were not allowed abaft the forward gangway, and were not troubled with visitors as no one cared to see the brave defenders. But we cared nothing about that so long as we were going towards home, and the accommodations were as good as we had been accustomed to having.

We reached Norwich about 2 a. m. on the 13th, and went aboard the cars, arriving at Worcester at 4 o'clock. At this hour Worcester people were still wrapt in the arms of Morpheus and of course we didn't meet with a very enthusiastic reception. Our little party formed on Foster street and noiselessly wended our way to the City Hall. A few stragglers who were around the depot reported our arrival and an hour after we received an invitation to go back to the depot refreshment room for lunch. This invitation was readily accepted and a famine was created in that refreshment room soon after our entrance. We had a good breakfast of hot coffee, cold meats, bread, pies, cakes, etc. After breakfast we returned to the hall to receive visitors, among the first of whom was Col. Pickett, who warmly welcomed us, shaking hands with all. We were right glad to see our colonel, and learn that he was getting the better of his wounds received at Cold Harbor.

By 8 o'clock the hall was filled, and welcoming speeches were made by his Honor Mayor Lincoln and others. After which it was proposed we make a parade and show ourselves over the city. This was objected to, not because we didn't wish to please our Worcester friends, but because we were sick and tired, and had had enough of parades and marches; our thoughts were of home and we were in a hurry to get there. Free tickets were furnished us on all the railroads, and we were dismissed for a week or until our muster out. I arrived home at noon, agreeably surprising my family, who were not expecting me for a week to come.

On the 20th of October we again met in Worcester for muster out and discharge papers. I was once more a free man, having been under the care and keeping of others a little more than thirty-seven months.

CLOSING SCENES.

Two months later we again met in Worcester to be paid off. This was to be our last meeting, henceforth we should travel in different paths and our meetings would be only by chance if ever. Shaking hands and wishing each other all manner of good fortune, we said our good-byes and parted. I have been through it and have had a great experience. I shall have no regrets that I did not go and have brought back no sorrowing memories. I have done what I could to preserve the union of the states. I have met the enemies of the country face to face, and done what I could to roll back the tide of rebellion, and if I have been of any little service to the country, I am glad of it. With all the officers of the regiment my relations have always been on the most amicable footing, and I am vain enough to believe that they will all bear me witness that I have always cheerfully obeyed all their commands and done all the duty required of me: that I have always treated them politely and shown them all the respect due their rank. In my little sports and jokes I have shown no partiality, and I trust there is no one who bears any malice towards me on that account. I have brought from the field no resentments or animosities towards any, but shall always hold in pleasing remembrance all, both living and dead, with whom I have been associated.

> Let him not boast who puts his armor on
> Like him who lays it off, his battle done.

THE END.

www.ingramcontent.com/pod-product-compliance
Lightning Source LLC
Chambersburg PA
CBHW030332170426
43202CB00010B/1104